Mor
Aι

phrasebook

Dan Bacon

with
**Abdennabi Benchehda &
Bichr Andjar**

Moroccan Arabic Phrasebook
1st edition

Published by
Lonely Planet Publications
Head Office: PO Box 617, Hawthorn, Victoria, 3122, Australia
US Office: PO Box 2001A, Berkeley, CA 94702, USA

Printed by
Singapore National Printers Ltd. Singapore

Published
February 1991

About This Book
This book was produced from an original manuscript by Dan Bacon, with the assistance of Abdennabi Benchehda and Bichr Andjar. Brahim Bouderka, Larbi Touaf, Youseff Yacoubi and Monsef Seraji assisted in proofreading. Sally Steward and Chris Taylor edited the book and Diana Saad typeset the Arabic script. Kathy Yates was responsible for the illustrations and Margaret Jung for design and front cover illustration.

National Library of Australia Cataloguing in Publication Data

Bacon, Dan
 Moroccan Arabic Phrasebook

 ISBN 0 86442 071 4

 1. Arabic language - Conversation and phrasebooks - English. 2. Arabic language - Dialects - Morocco. I. Title. (Series: Language Survival Kit)

492.783421
© Copyright Lonely Planet, 1991

Contents

Introduction

One of the first things you will notice about Morocco is its linguistic diversity. French, Berber, Modern Standard Arabic, as well as Moroccan Arabic, can all be heard in the major cities. This is due primarily to the rich historical past of the country. The Berbers, the original inhabitants, make up roughly half of the population, and the three major dialects of their language are widely spoken. When the Arabs came to Morocco in the 8th century they brought their language, which has evolved into the Moroccan Arabic of today. France officially entered the picture in 1912 when it began the Moroccan protectorate and French is still widely used in commerce and the educational system.

When one speaks of Arabic in Morocco there are two languages to be considered. On the one hand there is Modern Standard Arabic. This is the direct descendant of the language of the Koran and is understood throughout the contemporary Arab world. In Morocco it is used in newspapers, correspondence, news broadcasts and speeches but rarely in conversation. Moroccan Arabic, on the other hand, is the first language of the majority of Moroccans and really the most useful language to know when travelling in the country. It differs from Modern Standard Arabic to the extent that non-Moroccan speakers of Arabic, with the possible exception of Algerians and Tunisians, find it difficult to understand.

Moroccan Arabic is strictly a spoken language and rarely written down. When it is written, the Modern Standard Arabic script is used and therefore has been adopted in this book. It should prove useful to those who have had some previous exposure to Arabic as well as those wishing to make an attempt at learning the script. Also, if you cannot make yourself understood verbally, the script will be easily understood by Moroccans so you can point out the phrase you wish to communicate.

This phrasebook has been designed to provide the language you will need to survive as an independent traveller in Morocco. It is also an invaluable complement to the guidebook, *Morocco, Algeria & Tunisia – a travel survival kit*, published by Lonely Planet. Enjoy yourself and good luck!

Abbreviations Used in this Book

- (m) – male
- (f) – female
- (sg) – singular
- (pl) – plural
- (n) – noun
- (v) – verb

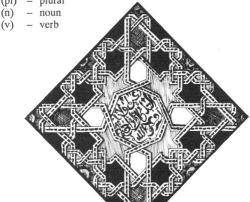

Pronunciation

The romanisation used in this book employs the English letters whose sounds come as close as possible to the corresponding sounds in Arabic. While there are quite a few similarities, several of the Arabic sounds will be new to the native English speaker and difficult at first to produce. Take comfort in the knowledge that perfect pronunciation is not necessary for you to be understood and that Moroccans are quite patient and willing to help.

Vowels
Long Vowels
a	as the 'a' in 'mad'
aa	as the 'a' in 'father'
ee	as the 'ee' in 'beet' or 'see'
ai	as the 'ai' in 'wait'
oo	as the 'oo' in 'boot'
o	as the 'o' in 'coke' or 'so'

Short Vowels
e	as the 'e' in 'glasses', very short
â	as the 'a' in 'at', very short
ô	as the 'u' in 'put', very short

Consonants

Many of the consonants are pronounced as in English. They include:

g	as the 'g' in 'go'
s	as the 's' in 'see'
sh	as the 'sh' in 'shine'
zh	as the 's' in 'pleasure'

Consonants Not Found in English

Here is where the English speaker can run into trouble. It is best to have a native speaker demonstrate these sounds.

'	a glottal stop; as the 'tt' sound in Cockney 'bottle'
q	similar to 'k', except pronounced further back in the throat
gh	similar to a French 'r'; may be approximated by gargling gently
H	similar to an English 'h', except pronounced deep in the throat with a loud raspy whisper – try whispering 'hey you' loudly from as deep in the throat as possible
"	may be approximated by saying the 'a' in 'fat' with the tongue against the bottom of the mouth and from as deep in the throat as possible
r	as the Spanish 'r' in 'para'
x	similar to 'gh', except without the musical buzz from the voice box; similar to the 'ch' in German 'bach'

Emphatic Consonants

The emphatic consonants, **d**, **s** and **t**, are pronounced with greater muscular tension in the mouth and throat and with a raising of the back of the tongue towards the roof of the mouth. This sensation can be approximated by prolonging the 'll' sound in pull. These consonants will be represented in bold in this book.

The letters **l**, **r**, and **z** can occasionally be pronounced emphatically and are indicated in the book by a double consonant. Note in particular 'God', *llah*.

Grammar

Obviously a comprehensive description of grammatical princi-
ples is not possible or even necessary here. Instead, enough of the
basics are provided to enable you to begin communicating in
Moroccan Arabic. Literal translations are provided when the
word order of the Arabic differs from the English.

Articles

In English the definite article is indicated by the word 'the'. The
definite article in Moroccan Arabic is expressed in one of two
ways depending on the first sound in the word. If the first letter
is *b, f, g, h, k, m, ', q, gh, H* or *"*, then *l* is pronounced at the
beginning of the word. If the word begins with *d, **d**, n, r, s, **s**,
sh, t, **t**, z*, or ***zh,*** then the initial letter is doubled.

   When making nouns and adjectives definite, the rule to follow
is: if the first letter of the word is made with the tip or front part
of the tongue then it is doubled. Otherwise place an *l* at the
beginning.

	Indefinite	**Definite**
bus	*kar*	*lkar*
paper, leaf	*werqa*	*lwerqa*
place	*blaasa*	*lblaasa*
house	***d**ar*	***dd**ar*
street	*zenqa*	*zzenqa*
price	*taman*	*ttaman*

One unique feature of Moroccan Arabic is that the definite article is used with adjectives as well as nouns. See the sections on Adjectives and Forming Sentences for examples.

Nouns

All nouns in Moroccan Arabic are either masculine or feminine. In general nouns ending in *a* are feminine while those ending with any other letter are masculine.

	Masculine		**Feminine**
morning	*sbaH*	food	*makla*
book	*ktab*	newspaper	*zhareeda*
beach	*bHer*	bed	*namooseeya*

Here are some of the exceptions:

evening	*msa* (m)	country	*blad* (f)
water	*lma* (m)	ring	*xatem* (f)
sun	*shemsh* (f)	hand	*yedd* (f)
road, way	*traiq* (f)	oil	*zeet* (f)

Forming the plural of nouns in Moroccan Arabic is more complicated than in English. Each singular noun has its own plural form which is usually difficult to predict. The two most common patterns used when forming plurals are adding *-een* to the end of masculine nouns and *-at* to feminine ones. There are many other patterns, so when learning words try to memorise the plural as well as the singular form.

	Singular	**Plural**
hand	*yedd*	*yeddeen*
inspector	*moofeteesh*	*moofeteesheen*
bed	*namooseeya*	*namooseeyat*

Adjectives

Adjectives follow nouns in the sentence and must agree in gender and number. That is, if a noun is feminine and singular then the adjective that follows it must be feminine and singular as well.

Feminine and plural forms of adjectives are derived from the masculine base form. The feminine form of the adjective is formed simply by adding *a*. The plural forms of adjectives, as with nouns, is difficult to predict. The two most common patterns are adding *-een* (eg 'pretty', *zween – zweeneen*) or replacing the long vowel sound in the middle of the word with *a* (eg 'big', *kbeer – kbar*).

the small bed	*nnamooseeya **ss**gheera*
	'the bed the small'
the small beds	*nnamooseeyat **ss**ghar*
	'the beds the smalls'

Comparative

The most common way of forming comparatives is to remove the long vowel from the regular adjective form (eg 'big' - *kbeer*, 'bigger' - *kber*).

He is bigger than my son.	*hoowa kber men weldee*
	'he bigger than son my'

Verbs

The vast majority of Moroccan Arabic verbs are made up of three-letter 'stems' (eg *gls* , 'to sit', and *rzh"* , 'to return') to which prefixes and suffixes are attached. The following is an example of the way the past, present and future tenses are formed for the verb *ktb* , 'to write', in which all three letters of the stem are consonants. Stems in which the middle or final letter is a vowel will differ slightly but this should give a general idea of how the verb structure works. It is not necessary to say the pronoun (I, we, you, etc) with the verb as in English; as every pronoun has a particular verb form, it is clear who is being referred to from the verb alone.

Past Tense

I wrote	*(kt)e(b)t*
you wrote	*(kt)e(b)tee*
he/it wrote	*(kt)e(b)*
she/it wrote	*(k)e(tb)at*
we wrote	*(kt)e(b)na*
you (pl) wrote	*(kt)e(b)too*
they wrote	*(k)e(tb)soo*

Present Tense

I write, am writing	*kan(kt)e(b)*
you (m) write, are writing	*kat(kt)e(b)*
you (f) write, are writing	*kat(k)e(tb)ee*
he/it writes, is writing	*kay(kt)e(b)*
she/it writes, is writing	*kat(kt)e(b)*
we write, are writing	*kan(k)e(tb)oo*
you (pl) write, are writing	*kat(k)e(tb)oo*
they write, are writing	*kay(k)e(tb)oo*

Future Tense

I will write	*ghadee n(kt)e(b)*
you (m) will write	*ghadee t(kt)e(b)*
you (f) will write	*ghadee t(k)e(tb)ee*
he/it will write	*ghadee ee(kt)e(b)*
she/it will write	*ghadee t(kt)e(b)*
we will write	*ghadee n(k)e(tb)oo*
you (pl) will write	*ghadee t(k)e(tb)oo*
they will write	*ghadee ee(k)e(tb)oo*

To Be

The Moroccan equivalent of 'to be' is not required in the present tense, except to express a recurring action (see the Forming Sentences section for examples). The use of the past tense, listed below, is similar to English except that it is not necessary to use the subject pronouns.

I was	*kônt*
you were	*kôntee*
he/it was	*kan*
she/it was	*kant*
we were	*kônna*
you were (pl)	*kôntoo*
they were	*kanoo*

I was sick yesterday.	*kônt mreed lbareH*
	'I was sick yesterday'
We were in Marrakech last week.	*kônna felmerraksh l'oosboo'' llee fat*
	'we were in Marrakech the week that passed'

To Have

'To have' is expressed in Moroccan Arabic by the preposition "ând-, literally 'in the possession of', followed by an object pronoun.

I have	"ândee
	'in my possession'
you have	"ândek
	'in your possession'
he/it has	"ândoo
	'in his/its possession'

she/it has	"ândha
	'in her/its possession'
we have	"ândna
	'in our possession'
you have (pl)	"ândkôm
	'in your possession'
they have	ândhôm
	'in their possession'

To Want/To Need

These two common expressions are communicated by placing two verbs next to each other in the sentence. Here are examples of each:

To Want

I want to go	bgheet nemshee
	'I want, I go'
you want to go	bgheetee temshee
	'you want, you go'
he wants to go	bgha yemshee
	'he wants, he goes'
she wants to go	bghat temshee
	'she wants, she goes'
we want to go	bgheena nemsheew
	'we want, we go'
you (pl) want to go	bgheetoo temsheew
	'you want, you go'
they want to go	bghaw yemsheew
	'they want, they go'

To Need

I need to go	*xessnee nemshee*
	'it is necessary for me, I go'
you need to go	*xessek temshee*
	'it is necessary for you, you go'
he needs to go	*xessoo yemshee*
	'it is necessary for him, he goes'
she needs to go	*xessha temshee*
	'it is necessary for her, she goes'
we need to go	*xessna nemsheew*
	'it is necessary for us, we go'
you (pl) need to go	*xesskôm temsheew*
	'it is necessary for you, you go'
they need to go	*xesshôm yemsheew*
	'it is necessary for them, they go'

Pronouns

Pronouns are divided into subject pronouns and object pronouns.

Subject Pronouns

I	*ana*	we	*Hna*
you (m)	*nta*	you (pl)	*ntooma*
you (f)	*ntee*		
he/it	*hoowa*	they	*hooma*
she/it	*heeya*		

Object Pronouns

me	*-ee*	us	*-na*
you	*-k*	you (pl)	*-kâm*
him/it	*-oo,h*	them	*-hâm*
her/it	*-ha*		

Rather than being separate words as in English, the object pronouns are attached to the end of other words in Moroccan Arabic.

he gave me	*"taanee*
to us, for us	*leena*

Possessive

Possession is most often expressed by the preposition *dyal-* followed by the appropriate object pronoun.

That shirt is mine.	*dak llqameezha dylee*
	'that the shirt belongs to me'
Her room is small.	*lbeet dyalha sgheera*
	'the room belonging to her small'

The possessives of certain nouns, particularly family members, are formed by attaching an object pronoun to the end of the noun.

my sister	*xetee*
	'sister my'
his friend	*saHboo*
	'friend his'

Forming Sentences

As mentioned in the Verbs section, the equivalent for the English verb 'to be' is normally not required in Moroccan Arabic when speaking in the present tense. In this type of sentence the subject usually comes first.

I am a teacher. *ana 'oosted*
 'I teacher'

That man is at the hotel. *dak rrazhel felootall*
 'that the man at the hotel'

A simple sentence can be formed using a noun with the definite article followed by an adjective without the definite article.

The view is beautiful. *lmender zween*
 'the view beautiful'

The bed is small. *nnamooseeya sgheera*
 'the bed small'

Where a verb is present, the subject of a sentence can be placed either before or after the verb. Remember that the subject pronouns are expressed by the appropriate verb form, so they don't need to be stated.

I went to the restaurant. *msheet llmet"âm*
 'I went to the restaurant'

The train left. *xerzhat lmasheena*
 'left the train'

Questions

A statement can be made into a question by either changing your voice inflection as in English or by preceding the statement with *wash*.

This wallet is mine.	*had lbeztaam dyalee*
	'this the wallet belonging to me'
Is this wallet mine?	*wash had lbeztaam dyalee?*
	'does this wallet belong to me'

Here are the main question words:

who	*shkoon*
Who is this girl?	*shkoon had lbent?*
	'who this the girl'
what	*ash*
What is that?	*ash dak shee?*
	'what that stuff'
when	*eemta*
When will it come?	*eemta ghadee eezhee?*
	'when going it come'
where	*feen*
Where is the bank?	*feen lbaanka?*
	'where the bank'
why	*"lash*
Why didn't he come?	*"lash mazhash?*
	'why not (he) come'

how	*keefash*
How did it come?	*keefash zha?*
	'how (it) came'
whose	*dyalmen*
Whose wallet is this?	*dyalmen had lbeztaam?*
	'whose this the wallet'
which	*ashmen*
Which room is ours?	*ashmen beet dyalna?*
	'which room ours'
how much	*shHal*
How much is it?	*shHal kayswa?*
	'how much it costs'

Negatives

A sentence can be made negative by placing *ma-* at the beginning of the verb and *-sh* at the end of it.

He came on time.	*zha felweqt*
	'he came on the time'
He didn't come on time.	*mazhash felweqt*
	'not he came on the time'

To form a negative sentence when there is no verb *mashee* can be used with the adjective.

The price is cheap.	*ttaman rxais*
	'the price cheap'
The price is not cheap.	*ttamam mashee rxais*
	'the price not cheap'

Prepositions

with, by, by means of	*b-, bee-*
from, than	*men-*
between	*been-, beenat-*
with	*m"a-*
without	*bla-*
before	*qbel-*
in front of, facing	*gôddam-*
after	*be"d-*
under, below	*teHt-*
of, belonging to	*d-,dyal-*
behind	*wra-*
in, among	*f-,fee-*
on	*"la-,"lee-*
over, above	*foq-*
next to	*Hda-*
to, for	*l-,lee-*

These prepositions do not occur separately but are fixed to the beginning of other words(eg 'the house' **dd**ar; 'in the house' *fe***dd**ar).

Conjunctions

or	*awla*
when, since	*mneen*
in order to	*bash*
and	*wô*
if	*eela, koon*
but	*walakeen*
until	*Hetta*
even though	*waxxa*
since	*mellee*

This & That

this	*had*
that (f)	*deek*
that (m)	*dak*
those	*dook*
this one (m)	*hada*
that one (m)	*hadak*
this one (f)	*hadl*
that one (f)	*hadeek*
these ones	*hadoo*
those ones	*hadook*
this thing, situation	*had shee*
that thing, situation	*dak shee*

this book	*had lektab*
	'this the book'
that girl	*deek lbent*
	'that the girl'
That (one) is very good.	*mezyan bezzaf hadak*
	'good very that one'

Greetings and Civilities

Greetings

When greeting Moroccans you'll find them more expressive than you may be accustomed to. One example of this is their liberal use of handshakes so remember it's polite to shake each person's hand when entering a room or encountering a group of people. If this becomes unrealistic, pronouncing the phrase *ssalamoo "leekm* is an acceptable substitute. Also notice that a handshake should be followed by placing your hand over your heart. It's common to greet close friends of the same sex by kissing them on both cheeks, especially if you haven't seen them recently.

The following phrases can be used when approaching someone you do not know. The first, *ssalamoo "leekm*, is universal throughout the Arab world and appropriate for greeting both one person and groups.

Peace be upon you. *ssalamoo "leekm*	السلام عليكم
Good morning. **s**baH lxaIr	صباح الخير
Good afternoon/evening. mselxaIr	مسا· الخير

The following phrases are less formal. They are spoken quickly, stringing several expressions together without necessarily waiting for a response.

24

How are you? ('No harm?')	لا باس؟
labas?	
How are you?	كيف حالك؟
keef Halek?	
Fine, thank you.	لا باس بارك اللّه فيك
labas, barak llahoo feek	
Is everything OK?	واش كل شي بخير؟
koolshee beexatr?	
Fine, praise God.	بخير الحمد للّه
beexatr lHamdoo llah	
What's happening?	اش خبارك؟
'ash xbarek?	
How are you doing?	
kee dayer? (m)	كي داير؟
kee dayra? (f)	كي دايرة؟
kee dayreen? (pl)	كي دايرين؟
Is your health OK?	الصحة لا باس؟
***sse*HHa labas?**	
Is your family OK?	العائلة لا باس؟
el"a'eela labas?	
Are your children OK?	الدرارى لا باس؟
ddraree labas?	

Goodbyes

The most common way to say goodbye is *bessalama*. Here are some other expressions to use when parting company:

Goodbye. ('with peace')	مع السلامة
m"a ssalama	
Goodbye. ('may God give you tranquility')	اللّه يهنيك
lla yhenneek	

May God help you. (to some
one who is going to work)
   lla y"awn

الله يعون

Good night. ('may God grant
you a good evening')
   lla ymseek "la xaɪr

الله يمسك على خير

Take care of yourself.
   thella frasek

تهلاّ فراسك

Civilities

Unlike English speakers, who tend to improvise when polite
remarks are required, Moroccans draw from a large number of
fixed expressions. The following are a few of the more common
ones, along with the contexts in which they are used. Though not
absolutely essential, these sayings will be greatly appreciated
when used correctly.

ensha'llah

انشا· الله

   If God wills. (talking about the future or making plans)

tbarka llah "leek

تباركة الله عليك

   The blessing of God upon you. (complimenting someone on
   an accomplishment)

lla ybarek feek

الله يبارك فيك

   May God bless you. (response to *tbarka llah "leek*)

lla yxlef

الله يخلف

   May God return it to you. (after receiving hospitality or getting
   paid)

bessaaHHtek

بالصحة

   To your health. (to someone after a haircut or bath)

lla y"taik saaHHa   الله يعطيك الصحة
   May God give you health. (response to *bessaaHHtek*)

lla ysehhel   الله يسهل
   May God make it easy for you. (to a beggar when not giving
   anything)

lla yrHem waldeek   الله يرحم والديك
   May God have mercy on your parents. (when asking or thank-
   ing someone for help)

"la salamtek   على سلامتك
   Peace upon you. (to someone arriving from a journey, recov-
   ering from an illness or calamity)

lla ysellemek   الله يسلمك
   May God grant you peace. (response to *"la salamtek*)

ttreq ssalama   طريق السلامة
   Have a peaceful trip. (to someone leaving on a journey)

besmeellah   بسم الله
   In the name of God. (before eating, travelling or any activity
   you wish to do in God's name)

Forms of Address

When addressing men, *aseedee*, 'sir', is a polite title and one appropriate to use with men in official positions. When used before a name it is shortened to *see* (eg *see Hameed*). A suitable expression to use when getting the attention of someone on the street or calling for the waiter in a cafe is *shreef*. The expression *see moHamed* can also be used in this way though it is not as polite. The frequently heard title *Hazh* (m), *Hazha* (f), is ascribed to one who has made the Muslim pilgrimage to Mecca.

Alalla, equivalent to 'madam', can be used when getting the attention of a woman or when addressing her in a conversation.

Some Useful Phrases

Yes.	ايه
eeyeh	
No.	لا
la	
OK.	وخة
waxxa	
Please.	عفاك
"*afak*	
Thank you.	
shkran	شكرا
barak llahoo feek	بارك الله فيك
Without honour. (response to thank you)	بلا جميل
bla zhmeel	
You don't need to thank me or my duty. (response to thank you)	لا شكرا على واجب
la shkran "la wezhb	

Excuse me. (apology)
    smeH leeya

اسمح لي

No problem. (response to
excuse me)
    makayn mooshkeel

ما كاين مشكل

Congratulations!
    mbrook!

مبروك

You are welcome at our
house.
    mreHba beek "ndna (sg)
    mreHba beekm "ndna (pl)

مرحب بك عندنا
مرحب بكم عندنا

Small Talk

You will probably find that in the main tourist areas you'll be approached by young Moroccans who have a working knowledge of at least three languages, and trying to start a conversation in Arabic will be a lost cause. Once away from these areas - especially Marrakesh and the north - it should be no problem getting into conversations with Moroccans. They are generally friendly, hospitable people and any effort you make at communicating in their language will be well received.

Meeting People

What is your name?
  asmeetek? — اسميتك ؟

My name is ...
  smeetee ... — سميتي...

I am honoured to meet you.
  metsherrfeen — متشرّفين

I would like to introduce you to ...
  bgheet nqeddemlek ... — بغيت نقدم لك...

Nationalities

Where are you from?
  mneen nta? (m) — منين انت؟
  mneen ntee? (f) — منين انت ؟
  mneen ntooma? (pl) — منين انتم ؟

30

I am from ...
  ana men ...
   America
  'amreeka
   Australia
  ostralya
   Canada
  kanada
   England
  anglateera
   France
  fransa
   Germany
  almaanya
   Italy
  'eetaaleeya
   Japan
  el yaban
   Morocco
  lmagreeb
   Netherlands
  holanda
   Spain
  eesbanya
   Sweden
  ssweed
   Switzerland
  sweesra

انا من...
امريكا
استراليا
كندا
انجلترا
فرنسا
المانيا
ايطاليا
اليابان
المغرب
هولاندا
اسبانيا
السويد
سويسرا

I am ...   ‫انا ...‬
  ana ...
    American
     meereekanee (m)   ‫مريكاني‬
     meereekaneeya (f)   ‫مريكانية‬
    Australian
     ostralee (m)   ‫استرالي‬
     ostraleeya (f)   ‫استرالية‬
    British
     negleezeeya (m)   ‫نجليزي‬
     negleezee (f)   ‫نجليزية‬
    French
     fransawee (m)   ‫فرنساوي‬
     fransaweeya (f)   ‫فرنساوية‬
    Italian
     'eetaalee (m)   ‫ايطالي‬
     'eetaaleeya (f)   ‫ايطالية‬
    Japanese
     lyabanee (m)   ‫ياباني‬
     lyabaneeya (f)   ‫يابانية‬
    Moroccan
     magreebee (m)   ‫مغربي‬
     magreebeeya (f)   ‫مغربية‬
    Spanish
     eesbanee (m)   ‫اسباني‬
     eesbaneeya (f)   ‫اسبانية‬
    Sweden
     sweedee (m)   ‫سويدي‬
     sweedeeya (f)   ‫سويدية‬
    Swiss
     sweesree (m)   ‫سويسري‬
     sweereeya (f)   ‫سويسرية‬

Age

How old are you?	شحال ف عمرك؟
shHal f"merek?	

I am ...	عندي..
"ândee ...	
18 years old	تمنطاشل عام
tmentaashal "am	
25 years old	خمسة وعشرين عام
xamsa oo"shreen	
"am	

Note: See the Numbers chapter for your particular age.

Occupations

What is your occupation?	اش كتعمل؟
ash kat"mel? (m)	اش كتعملي؟
ash kat"âmlee? (f)	

I am a/an ...	انا...
ana	
businessperson	
*ta**zh**er* (m)	تاجر
*ta**zh**ra* (f)	تاجرة
carpenter	
*na**zhzh**ar*	نجار
doctor	
tbeeb (m)	طبيب
tbeeba (f)	طبيبة
engineer/architect	
moohendees (m)	مهندس
moohendeesa (f)	مهندسة

government employee
 mweddef (m)   موظف
 mweddefa (f)   موظفة
journalist
 saaHaafee (m)   صحافي
 saaHaafeeya (f)   صحافية
lawyer
 mooHamee (m)   محامي
 mooHameeya (f)   محامية
retiree
 qebt lantreet   قبطت لانتريت
secretary
 kateeb (m)   كاتب
 kateeba (f)   كاتبة
student
 taaleb (m)   طالب
 taaleba (f)   طالبة
teacher
 'oostad (m)   استاد
 'oostada (f)   استادة

Religion

What is your religion?   أشنو هو دين ديالك؟
ashnoo hoowa deen dyalek?

I am …   انا …
 ana …
  Buddhist
   boodee (m)   بودي
   boodeeya (f)   بودية

Christian
  maseeHee (m)
  maseeHeeya (f)
Hindu
  hendee (m)
  hendeeya (f)

مسيحي
مسيحية

هندي
هندية

Jewish اهودي
  eehoodee (m) اهودية
  eehoodeeya (f)
Muslim مسلم
  meslem (m) مسلمة
  meslema (f)

Family

This is my...
  hada ... (m) هادا ...
  hadee ... (f) هادى ...
    wife مراتي
     mratee
    husband رجلي
     *ra**zh**lee*
    brother خوى
     xoya
    sister
     xôtee
    mother مي ، والدة ديالي
     mmwee, waleeda
     dyalee
    father با ، والد ديالي
     bba, waleed dyalee
    parents والدىّ
     waldeeya
    son ولدى
     weldee
    daughter بنتي
     bentee
    friend صاحبي
     saaHebee (m) صاحبتي
     saaHebtee (f)

Are you married?
wash nta mzhoowzh? (m)
was ntee mzhoowzha? (f)
واش انت مجوج ؟
واش انت مجوجة؟

I am married.
ana mzhoowzh (m)
ana mzhoowzha (f)
انا مجوج
انا مجوجة

I am not married.
ana mashee mzhoowzh (m)
ana mashee mzhoowzha (f)
انا ماشي مجوج
انا ماشي مجوجة

Do you have any children?
wash "ândek loowlad?
واش عندك لولاد ؟

I don't have any children.
m"ândeesh Hetta shee loowlad
ما عنديش حتى شي لولاد

How many children do you have?
shHal men weld "ândek?
شحال من ولد عندك؟

I have ...
"ândee ...
عندى...

    one son
     waHed lweld
واحد الولد

    one daughter
     waHed lbent
واحد البنت

    two sons
     zhoozh dyal loowlad
جوج ديال الولاد

    two daughters
     zhoozh dyal lbnat
جوج ديال البنات

Feelings

I am ...
  ana ...
    bored
      meqnot (m)
      meqnotaa (f)
    happy
      ferHan (m)
      ferHana (f)
    scared
      xayf (m)
      xayfa (f)
    sick
      mreed (m)
      mreedaa (f)
    tired
      "eyyan (m)
      "eyyana (f)
    upset/angry
      mqelleq (m)
      mqellqa (f)

انا...

مقنوط
مقنوطة

فرحان
فرحانة

خايف
خايفة

مريض
مريضة

عيان
عيانة

مقلق
مقلقة

I am hungry.
  feeya zhoowâ"

في" جوعة

I am thirsty.
  feeya l"atesh

في" العطش

Language Problems

I don't speak Arabic.
  makan"refsh l"ârbeeya

ماكنعرفش العربية

I only know a little Arabic.
  kan"ref gheer shee shweeya
  dyal l"ârbeeya

كنعرف غير شي شوية
ديال العربية

Do you speak English?
  wash kat"ref
  negleezeeya?

واش كتعرف نجليزية ؟

Does anyone here speak
English?
  wash kayn shee Hedd
  henna lee kay"ref
  negleezeeya?

واش كاين شي حدّ هنا لي
كيعرف نجليزية ؟

I understand.
  fhemt

فهمت

I don't understand.
  mafhemtsh

مافهمتش

Do you understand?
  wash fhemtee?

واش فهمتي ؟

What did you say?
  ash gôltee?

اش جلتي ؟

How do you say ... in
Arabic?
  keefash katgooloo ...
  bel"ârbeeya?

كيفاش كتجولو ...
ب العربية؟

What does this mean?
  ash kat"ânee hadee?

اش كتعني هادي؟

Please speak slowly!
  tkellem beshweeya
  "afak!

تكلم بشوية عفاك

Translate this word for me
please.
  terzhemlee had lkalma
  "afak

ترجم لي هاد الكلمة عفاك

Write it down for me.	كتبها لي
ktebhaleeya	
Please repeat it.	عودها عفاك
"âwwedha "afak	

Some Useful Phrases

Where are you going?	فين غادى؟
feen ghadee?	
Watch out!	
"ândak!	عنداك!
balek!	بالك!
Be careful.	رد بالك
redd balek	
It is clear/understood/agreed upon.	صافي
saafee	
Look!	شوف!
shoof!	
Listen!	سمع!
smâ"!	
I'm ready.	
ana moozhood (m)	انا موجود
ana moozhooda (f)	انا موجودة
Not yet.	
mazel	مازال
baaqee	باقي
Hurry up!	سربي!
serbee!	
Slow down!	ب شوية عليك!
beshweeya "leek!	
Go away!	سير في حالك!
seer fHalek!	

That doesn't interest me.
*dakshee may-
hemmneesh*
داك شي ميهمنيش

Leave me alone.
"talnee tteesa"
عطيني التيساع

Leave us alone.
"taina tteesa"
عطينا التيساع

Get away from me.
bâ""âd mennee
بعد مني

too much/a lot
bezzaf
بزٲف

a little
shweeya
شوية

Yes I can.
eeyeh nqder
ايه نقدر

No I can't.
la manqdersh
لا مانقدرش

It is possible.
yemken
يمكن

It is not possible.
mayemkensh
ما يمكنش

not important
mashee mooheem
ماشي

very important
mooheem bezzaf
مهم بزاف

I forgot.
nseet
نسيت

Accommodation

Hotels in Morocco are generally well furnished and reasonably priced. The majority are ranked using the European star system from one star (least expensive) to five star (most expensive). The prices of ranked hotels, except five star, are established by the government and are required by law to be posted. A list of all hotels and campsites is given free of charge by the national tourist offices located in major cities.

When looking for accommodation you may be offered assistance by unofficial guides and using a few Arabic phrases is a good way to let them know whether you need their services or not.

Finding Accommodation

Where is ...?	فـين كـاين ... ؟
feen kayn ...?	
a hotel	شـي اوطـيل
shee ootail	
a Youth Hostel	اوبـرج
'ooberzh	دار الـشـبـاب
daar shshabab	
a campsite	شـي مخـيم
shee môxeyyem	

Where is an inexpensive hotel?	فـين كـاين شـي اوطـيل رخـيص؟
feen kayn shee ootail	
rxals?	

Where is a nice hotel?
  feen kayn shee ootail mezyan?

فين كاين شي اوطيل مزيان ؟

I've already found a hotel.
  ana lgeet shee 'ootail men qbel

انا لقيت شي اوطيل من قبل

Please take me to a hotel.
  wesselnee l shee ootail "afak

وصلني ل شي اوطيل عفاك

At the Hotel
Checking In

Is there a room available?
  wash kayn shee beet xaweeya?

واش كاين شي بيت خاوية ؟

What is the price of the room?
  shHal ttaman dyal lbeet?

شحال التمن ديال البيت؟

Is breakfast included?
  wash lftor mHsoob m"a lbeet?

واش الفطور محسوب مع البيت؟

Which floor?
  ashmen tebqa?

اش من طبقة ؟

I'd like a room ...
  bgheet shee beet ...

بغيت شي بيت...

  for one person
    dyal waHed

ديال واحد

  for two people
    dyal zhoozh

ديال جوج

  with a bathroom
    belHâmmam

ب الحمام

with a shower
beddoosh

ب الدوش

with hot water
belma sxoon

ب الما سخون

Can I see the room?
wash yemkenlee nshoof lbeet?

واش يمكن لي نشوف البيت؟

This room is good.
had lbeet mezyana

هاد البيت مزيانة

I don't like this room.
ma"âzhbatneesh had lbeet

ما عجباتنيش هاد البيت

Is there a room available
which is ... than this one?
was kayn shee beet ... men hadee?

واش كاين شي بيت...
من هادي؟

bigger
kber

كبر

smaller	صغر
sgher	
cheaper	رخص
rxe**s**	
better	حسن
Hessen	

I am going to stay for ...	غادي نجلس...
ghadee ngles ...	
one day	واحد نهار
waHed nhar	
two days	يومين
yoomayn	
one week	واحد الاسبوع
waHed l'oosboo"	

During Your Stay

Could we have an extra bed?	واش يمكن لك تزيد لينا
wash yemkenlek	واحد النّاموسية؟
tzeedleena waHed	
nnamooseeya?	

Please bring me	جيب لي عفاك...
zheeblee ... "afak	
a towel	واحد الفوطة
waHed lfota	
a blanket	واحد البطانية
waHed lbtaaneeya	
breakfast	الفطور
lftor	

Which room is ours?
  ashmen beet dyalna?

اش من بيت ديالنا ؟

Please give me the room key.
  *"taïnee ssaaroot dyal
  beet "afak*

عطيني الساروت ديال البيت
عفاك

Where can I wash my clothes?
  *feen yemkenlee
  nsebben Hwayezhee?*

فين يمكن لي نصبن حوايجي؟

Please clean the room now.
  *neddeflee lbeet daba
  "afak*

نضف لي البيت دابا عفاك

Can I make a telephone call?
  *wash yemkenlee n"mel
  telefon?*

واش يمكن لي نعمل تلفون ؟

Checking Out

We would like to check out ...
  bgheena nemsheew ...

بغينا نمشيو...

  now
    daba

دابا

  at noon
    fettnash

ف الطناش

  tomorrow
    ghedda

غدا

  tomorrow morning
    ghedda fessbaH

غدا ف الصباح

Please prepare our bill.
  *wezhzhedleena lHsab
  dyalna "afak*

وجد لينا الحساب عفاك

Can I pay by ...?
wash yemkenlee
*nxelle***s*b ...?*
 travellers' cheque
  shek seeyaHee
 credit card
  kaart kreedee

واش يمكن لي نخلص ب...؟

شيك سياحي

كارت كريدى

Can I leave my things here until ...?
واش يمكن لي نخلي الحوايج ديالي هنا حتى ... ؟
wash yemkenlee nxellee lHawezh dyalee henna Hetta ...?

  this afternoon
  هاد العشية
   had l"sheeya

  this evening
  اليوم بالليل
   lyoom beleel

Call me a taxi please.
عيطلي على واحد الطاكسي عفاك
"yyetlee "la waHed ttaaxee "afak

Where is the laundry?
فين كاينة شي مصبنة ؟
feen kayna shee mesbana?

Please ... this/these for me.
  "afak ... leeya hada (m)
عفاك ... لي هادا
  "afak ... leeya hadee (f)
عفاك ... لي هادى
  "afak ... leeya hadoo (pl)
عفاك ... لي هادو

  wash
  صبن
   sebben

  iron
  صلح
   sleH

  sew
  خيط
   xeyyet

When will it be ready?
امت غادى تكون موجودة ؟
'emta gadee takoon moozhooda?

I need it ...
  ana meHtazh beeha ...
    today
      lyoom
    tomorrow
      gedda

انا محتاج بيها ...
اليوم
غدا

I need it quickly.
  ana zerban beeha
This isn't mine.
  hadee mashee dyalee
Is the laundry ready?
  wash lHwayezh
  wazhdeen?

انا زربان بيها
هادى ماشي ديالي
واش الحوايج واجدين؟

Some Useful Words

address
  "ônwan
air-conditioning
  klemateezaseeyon
arrival
  wsol
ashtray
  tfaya
bathtub
  Hâmmam
bedroom
  beet nn"as
blanket
  bttaaneeya
chair
  koorsee

عنوان
كليمتيزسيون
وصول
تفاية
حمام
بيت النعاس
بطانية
كورسي

clean *nqee*	نقي
cost *taman*	تمن
crowded *zHam*	زحام
curtain *xameeya*	خامية
dinner *"sha*	عشا
dirty *mwessex*	موسخ
door *bab*	باب
electricity **do**	ضو
empty *xawee*	خاوى
food *makla*	مكلة

full	عامر
"amer	
light bulb	بولة
boola	
lift (n)	سنسور
sensoor	
lock	قفل
qfel	
mirror	مراية
mraya	
noise	صداع
sda"	
pillow	مخدة
mxedda	
quiet	مهدّن
mhedden	
sheet	ازار
eezar	
sleep	نعسة
nâ"sa	
soap	صابون
saaboon	
spend the night	بات
bat	
stairs	دروج
*droo**zh***	
suitcase	باليزة
baleeza	
toilet	بيت الما
beet lma	
window	شرجم
*sher**zh**em*	

Getting Around

Public transportation in Morocco is both inexpensive and easy to use. Within city limits one can take either city buses or small (petit) taxis.

For trips between major cities trains are the quickest and most comfortable means of travel, though they can be crowded at certain times of the year. The other options are buses and large (grand) taxis. The buses are the cheapest choice but can vary quite a bit in both speed and comfort. With grand taxis it is possible to pay on a per-seat basis as well as for the entire taxi.

Finding Your Way

Where is ...?
feen ...?
فـين... ؟

  the city bus station
    kayna mHetta dyal
    ttobeesat
كاينة المحطة ديال الطوبيسات

  the inter-city bus station
    kayna mHetta dyal
    lkeeran
كاينة المحطة ديال الكيران

  the train station
    kayn lagaar
كاين لجار

  the airport
    kayn lmaataar
كاين المطار

  the taxi stand
    kayna blaasa dyal
    ttaakseeat
كاينة البلاصة ديال التكسيات

What ... is this?	اش من ... هادى؟
ashmen ... hadee?	
city	مدينة
mdeena	
street	زنقة
zenqa	
boulevard	شارع
sharee"	

What time does ... leave?	فوقاش كيخرج ... ؟
fooqash kayxrezh ...? (m)	فوقاش كتخرج... ؟
fooqash katxrezh ...? (f)	
the bus (city)	الطوبيس
ttobees	
the bus (inter-city)	الكار
lkar	
the train	الماشينة
lmasheena	
the taxi	الطكسي
ttaaksee	
the plane	الطيارة
ttalyyara	

Directions

Go straight ahead!	سير نيشان!
seer neeshan!	
Turn right!	ضور عل ليمن!
dor "âl leemen	
Turn left!	ضور عل ليسر!
dor "âl leeser	

Go backwards!	رجع لور
rzhâ" lor!	
Continue on a little further!	زيد قدام واحد شوية !
zeed qeddem waHed	
shweeya!	
How far?	شحال بعيد ؟
shHal b"aid?	
north	شمال
shamel	
south	جنوب
zhanoob	
east	شرق
sherq	
west	غرب
gherb	

Air

Air fares in Morocco are controlled by the national airline, Royal Air Maroc. It is the only company that offers internal flights and, while quite reasonable by international standards, is expensive compared to the other means of transportation available. If you need to be somewhere in a hurry, however, air travel is worth checking out.

When is there a flight to …?	امتى غادي تكون شي
'emta gadee tkoon shee	طيارة ل ... ؟
tayyara l… ?	
I'd like a … ticket to Casa-blanca please.	عفاك بغيت واحد البيي
"afak bgeet waHed	ل الدار البيضا'...
lbeyyee l ddar lbaida …	

return
  *bash nemshee oo
  nzhee*

باش نمشي و نجي

1st class
  ddarazha lloola

الدرجة اللولة

2nd class
  ddarazha ttaneeya

الدرجة التانية

What is the fare?
  shHal taman lbeyee?

شحال تمن البيي ؟

What time do I need to be at
the airport?
  *'ashmen sa'a xessnee
  nkoon felmataar?*

اش من ساعة خصني نكون
ف المطار ؟

Bus

Give ('tear') me two tickets
to ... plcasc.
  *qettâ"lee zhoozh dyal
  lwraq l ... "afak*

قطع لي جوج ديال الوراق ل ...
عفاك

What time does the first/last
bus leave?
  *fooqash kayxrezh lkar
  lewwel/laxer?*

فوقاش كيخرج الكار
الاول/الاخر؟

Where is this bus going?
  feen ghadee had lkar?

فين غادي هاد الكار؟

Is this bus going to ...?
  wash had lkar ghadee l ...?

واش هاد الكار غادي ل ... ؟

How much is it for a ticket
from here to ...?
  *shHal kat"mel lwerqa
  bash nemshee men
  henna l ...?*

شحال كتعمل الورقة باش
نمشي من هنا ل... ؟

Which bus is going to …?
  ashmen kar ghadee l …?

اش من كار غادي ل … ؟

Where can I catch a bus to …?
  *feen yemkenlee nqbed
  lkar l …?*

فين يمكن لي نقبض الكار ل … ؟

When is the bus going to come?
  *'eemta ghadee eezhee
  lkar?*

امتى غادي يجي الكار ؟

How many buses per day go
to …?
  *shHal men kar
  kaymshee l … fenhar?*

شحال من كار كيمشي ل …
ف النهار ؟

Is … far from here?
  *wash … b"ald men
  henna?*

واش   بعيد من هنا ؟

Is … near here?
  wash … qreeb l henna?

واش   قريب ل هنا ؟

Please tell me when we
arrive at …
   "afak eela wselna l …
   goolhaleeya

عفاك الى وصلنا ل...
جولها لي

Train

Is this train going to …?
   wash had lmasheena
   ghadeeya l …?

واش هاد الماشينة غادية ل... ؟

Please give me two 1st/2nd
class tickets.
   "afak qettâ"lee zhoozh
   lweraq dyal daaraazha
   lewwla/taneeya

عفاك عطيني جوج الوراق
ديال درجة لولة/ثانية

Is this seat free?
   wash had lblaasa
   xaweeya?

واش هاد البلاصة خاوية ؟

This seat is taken.
   had lblasa "âmra

هاد البلاصة عامرة

Would you mind if I opened
the window?
   makayn mooshkeel eela
   Hleet sserzhem?

ماكاين مشكل الى حليت
السرجم ؟

Where do I need to change
trains?
   feen xessnee nbeddel
   lmasheena?

فين خصني نبدل الماشينة ؟

Taxi

Is there a taxi stand near here?
   wash kayn shee blaasa
   dyal ttakseeat qreeb l
   henna?

واش كاين شي بلاصة ديال
التكسيات قريب ل هنا ؟

Go slowly please.
   temsha bshweeya "afak
تمشا ب شوية عفاك

Stop here please.
   wqef henna "afak
وقف هنا عفاك

I would like to get out here please.
   bgheet nenzel henna "afak
بغيت ننزل هنا عفاك

Take me to ...
   wesselnee l ...
وصلني ل ...

   this address
     had l"ônwen
هاد العنوان

   the airport
     lmaataar
المطار

   the bank
     lbaanka
البانكة

I'm in a hurry.
   ana zerban (m)
   ana zerbana (f)
انا زربان
انا زربائة

Please wait for me.
   tsennanee "afak
تسنّاني عفاك

I'll be right back.
   daba nzhee
دابا نجي

Stop!
   'ooqef!
اوقف !

Some Useful Words

bicycle
   beshkleetaa
بشكليطة

boulevard
   sharee"
شارع

car طوموبيل
  tomobeel

corner قنت
  qent

dirt road بيست
  peest

early بكرى
  bekree

early in the morning ف الصباح بكرى
  fssbaaH bekree

hurry up سربي
  serbee

late معطل
  m"ettel

motorcycle/moped *motor*	موطور
on time *felweqt*	ف الوقت
petrol *leesans*	ليصانص
hire *kra*	كرا
slow down *beshweeya "leek*	ب شوية عليك
stop light ***do** lHmer*	ضو الحمر
stop sign *stop*	سطوب
street *zenqa*	زنقة

Around Town

The quickest way to get oriented in a Moroccan city is to head directly for the local tourist office. They are normally located in the centre of town and offer free city maps indicating the main municipal buildings and tourist sites.

When looking for a particular address you could run into trouble. Often streets and numbers are unmarked and many street names, especially in Casablanca and Rabat, have recently been changed from French to Arabic. The best bet is to ask a local shop owner if you suspect the address is nearby. If all else fails, the unofficial experts in giving directions are the small (petit) taxi drivers.

Where is ...?
feen ...? | فـين ... ؟
| a bank | كاينة شي بانكة
| *kayna shee baanka* |
| the post office | كاينة البوسطة
| *kayna lboostaa* |
| the police station | كاينة الكوميسارية
| *kayna lkoomeesareeya* |
| the town hall | كاينة البلدية
| *kayna lbaladeeya* |
| a barber | كاين شي حلاق
| *kayn shee Hellaq* |
| the market | كاين المارشي
| *kayn lmarshay* |
| the open air market | كاين السوق
| *kayn ssooq* |

the ... embassy *kayna sseefara dyal ...*	كاينة السيفارة ديال...
the ... consulate *kayna lqonsoleeya dyal ...*	كاينة القنصلية ديال...
the old city *kayna lmdeena lqdeema*	كاينة المدينة القديمة
a laundry *kayna shee msebb- ana*	كاينة شي مصبنة

How far is ...? *shHal b"aid ...?*	شحال بعيد... ؟
I am looking for the ... *kanqelleb "la ...*	كنقلب على ...
What time do they open? *weqtash kayHelloo?*	وقتاش كيحلو؟
What time do they close? *weqtash kayseddoo?*	وقتاش كيسدّو ؟
Are they still open? *wash mazel Haleen?*	واش مازال حالين ؟

At the Post Office

Stamps are available at tobacco stands in addition to the post office. It is best to mail your letters at the mail slots outside post offices as pick-ups can be infrequent at other mail boxes. Sending packages out of the country is fairly straight forward although you will be required to fill out a customs declaration form. Be sure to leave the package open because an official is required to see the contents before it is sealed.

For telephone calls, phone booths located throughout major cities are far and away the best choice. For anything other than local calls they are much cheaper than hotels and always quicker than the post office. Reverse charges calls can be made either from a hotel or the phone section of the post office. State that you wish to call 'PCV' and provide your name as well as the name, city, country and number of the person you are calling.

I would like to ...	...بغيت
bgheet ...	
buy some stamps	نشرى شي تنابر
nshree shee tnaber	
send a telegram	نصيفط واحد التيليجرام
nsaifet waHed	
tteeleegram	

send a package
  n*saifet* waHed
  lkooleeya
	نصيفط واحد الكولية

send this registered mail
  n*saifet* hadee
  recoomaanday
	نصيفط هادى ركومائدى

make a phone call n"mel ttelefoon	نعمل التلفون
make a reverse charges phone call n"mel ttelefoon PCV	نعمل التلفون بي سي في

How much is it to send this to …?
  bshHal ghadee
  n*saifet*hadee l …?
	ب شحال غادى نصيفط
	هادى ل... ؟

How much is it to send a post
card to the USA?
  bshHal ghadee
  n*saifet* waHed lkart
  postaal lamreeka?
	ب شحال غادى نصيفط واحد
	الكارت بوسطال ل أمريكا ... ؟

I want to send this … bgheet n*saifet*hadee …	بغيت نصيفط هادى...
air mail bettaiyyaara	ب الطيارة
surface post "adeeya	عادية

Please give me a receipt. "tainee faktora "afak	عطيني فاكتورة عفاك

Has any mail come for me?
  wash zhawleeya shee
  braawat?
	واش جاو لي شي براوات ؟

Some Useful Words

box	صندوق
sendoq	
breakable	يقدر يتهرس
eeqder eetherres	
cardboard box	كارطونة
kartoona	
customs official	ديواني
deewaanee	
envelope	جوى
***zh**wa*	
glue	لصاق
***l**saaq*	
inspector	مفتيش
moofetteesh	
insurance	لاصورانص
*laasoraan**s***	
mailman	فاكتور
faktor	
number	رقم
raqem	
wrapping paper	كاغيت
kagheet	
phone stall in post office	بيت
beet	
stamp	تانبر
tanber	
string	قنبة
qennba	
tape	سكاتش
skaatsh	

At the Bank

After bargaining for almost every purchase you will be pleased to know that currency exchange rates are fixed by the government and will be the same wherever you change money. Rates are posted although a few banks have started charging a Dr 5 fee per travellers' cheque.

Banking hours for most of the year are 8.30 to 11.30 am and 2.15 to 4.15 pm. During Ramadan (the Muslim month of fasting) and summer months the hours change to 8.15 am to 1.45 pm. At times other than these money can be changed at the international airports and most major hotels.

The dirham, Morocco's currency, cannot be exchanged once out of the country. Save your exchange receipts because you can change a percentage back into foreign currency at the airport when you leave.

I would like to exchange some money. *bgheet nserref shee floos*	بغيت نصرف شي فلوس
Has my money arrived yet? *wash zhaw lfloos dyalee awla mazel?*	واش جاو الفلوس ديالي أولا ما زال ؟
Where should I sign? *feen xessnee nweqqe"?*	فين خصني نوقع ؟
Can I have money transferred here from my bank? *wash yemken llbanka dyalee tsalfet shee floos lhenna?*	واش يمكن ل البانكة ديالي تصيفط شي فلوس ل هنا ؟

How long will it require for
the money to arrive?
shHal dyal weqt
kayxess lfloos bash
eewseloo?

شحال ديال الوقت كيخص
الفلوس باش يوصلو؟

Some Useful Words

banknotes
wraq

cash window
sendoq

وراق

صندوق

change	صرف
serf	
money	فلوس
floos	
travellers' cheque	شيك السياحي
shek seeyaHee	

Emergencies

Your first choice in a health emergency or theft should be to look for a major intersection where a policeman will probably be stationed. If this is not possible ask a local shopkeeper with a phone to make the appropriate call for you.

Call the police!	عيط البوليس!
"eyyet lboolees!	
Call a doctor!	عيط الطبيب!
"eyyet ltbeeb!	
Help me please!	عاوني عفاك!
"awennee "afak!	
Thief!	شفار!
sheffaar!	
They robbed me!	شفروني!
shefferoonee!	

In the Country

Weather

How is the weather there?
kee dayer lzhoow dyal temma?

كي داير الجو ديال تما ؟

Is it ... there?
wash ... temma?

واش ... تما ؟

   hot
     kayn ssehd

كاين الصهد

   cold
     kayn lberd

كاين البرد

   raining
     kayna shta

كاينة الشتا

   snowing
     kayn ttelzh

كاين التلج

   windy
     kaysot rreeH

كاينة الريح

   cloudy
     kayna ddbaaba

كاينة الضبابة

What is the temperature today?
shHal feddaaraazhat dyal Harara lyoom?

شحال ف الدرجة ديال الحرارة اليوم ؟

What is the weather going to be like today?
keefash ghadee eekoon lzhoow lyoom?

كيفاش غادى يكون الجو اليوم ؟

Geographical Terms

beach
  laplaazh

desert
  seHra

island
  zhazeera

lake
  daya

mountain
  zhbel

ocean
  bHar

river
  wad

road
  traiq

لبلاج

صحرا

جزيرة

ضاية

جبل

بحر

واد

طريق

rock *Hezhra*	حجرة
sand *remla*	رملة
valley *wad*	واد
waterfall *kaskad*	كسكاد

Animals & Insects

bee *nehla*	نحلة
bird *tair*	طير
camel *zhmel*	جمل
cat *meshsh*	مش
chicken *dzhazha*	دجاجة
cockroach *serraq zzeet*	سراق الزيت
cow *begra*	بجرة
dog *kelb*	كلب
donkey *Hmar*	حمار
fish *Hoota*	حوتة

fly	دبّانة
debbana	
goat	معزة
me"za	
horse	عود
"âwd	
monkey	قرد
qerd	
mule	بغل
beghl	

pig *Helloof*	حلوف
rooster *ferroozh*	فرّوج
sheep *Hawlee*	حاولي
snake *Hensh*	حنش
wild animal *Hayawan*	حيوان

Camping

Where is the campground? *feen kayn lmôxeyyem?*	فين كاين المخيم ؟
Is it OK for us to camp here? *makayn mooshkeel eela xeyyemna henna?*	ما كاين مشكل الا خيمنا هنا ؟

Some Useful Words

agriculture *feelaHa*	فلاحة
bridge *qentra*	قنطرة
countryside *badeeya*	بادية
dirt *traab*	تراب
flower *noowwara*	نوّرة
forest *ghaba*	غابة

grass
  rbee"
  ربيع

historical ruins
  l'aataarat
  اثار

moon
  gmra
  جمرة

mosque
  zhame"
  جامع

mud
  ghees
  غيس

plant
  nbat
  نبات

rose
  werda
  ورضة

star
  nezhma
  نجمة

sun
  shemsh
  شمس

tree
  shezhra
  شجرة

village
  dwaar
  ضوار

Food

Moroccan Specialities

Moroccan cuisine is delicious, visually striking, and varied. Here are some highlights of the country's rich culinary tradition:

taazheen   طجين

A thick and richly spiced stew named for the round dish with a cone-shaped cover in which it is prepared. Traditionally lamb or mutton, *taazheen* can also be made of beef, fish or poultry. Some of the most popular are lamb with prunes and onions, chicken with lemon, chicken with almonds and hard boiled eggs, and meatballs with eggs. The best are cooked over a charcoal brazier. In homes *taazheen* is eaten from the dish in which it is cooked, placed in the centre of a low round table and eaten by hand with bread.

kooskoos or *seksoo*   سكسو

This, the most popular meal in North Africa, consists of steamed semolina grain covered with a savoury meat and vegetable sauce. *Kooskoos* actually refers to the semolina grain, initially rolled by hand but now available dried and packaged. Again, an almost infinite number of variations are available. Two of the best are lamb with vegetables, most often including carrots, turnips, cabbage, pumpkin and squash; and lamb with raisins and onions. Customarily *kooskoos* is eaten by hand, rolling it into a ball and popping it in your mouth. This is really an art and much more difficult than it looks. You might want to give it a try, but be sure to keep a spoon handy!

75

bestaila بسطيلة

This is the well-known Moroccan delicacy made of chicken or pigeon, eggs, almonds, sugar and saffron, stuffed between many layers of a crisp, paper-thin pastry. A must when visiting the country, *bestaila* can be specially ordered from many neighbourhood bakeries as well as the best Moroccan restaurants.

meshwee مشوى

Often found at weddings and other important occasions, *meshwee* is a complete lamb roasted and served in the centre of a table. Guests pull pieces of meat off with their hands and eat them with bread.

Hareera حريرة

A thick, filling soup of tomatoes, lentils, chick-peas and meat seasoned with coriander and lemon. Traditionally used to break the fast during Ramadan, the Muslim month of fasting, *Hareera* is now available at most Moroccan restaurants all year round. You will be surprised by both its unique flavour and inexpensive price. A bowl of this delicious soup with bread sells for Dr 1 in the famous Jemaa El Fena of Marrakesh.

atay benna"na اتاى ب النعناع

Mint tea in Morocco is not only a drink but a national institution, practised thousands of times a day in settings from Berber tents in the High Atlas to the King's Palace. Made with mint, green tea and sugar, each step in the preparation process appears carefully calculated, having been refined by countless repetitions. Expect many opportunities to experience the tea ritual first hand while staying in the country.

One of the most important ingredients of the national cuisine is the gracious and hospitable atmosphere of the Moroccan home. It is indeed a tragedy that this cannot be duplicated in a restaurant. If you should have the pleasure of being invited for a meal, here are some things to keep in mind. First, shoes are not normally worn inside so you will be expected to remove yours before stepping on any carpets. Don't worry about washing your hands, your host will bring a basin with water to you while you are seated. Once the host pronounces *besmeellah*, 'in the name of God', the meal will begin with everyone eating out of a common dish with their hands or, if *kooskoos* is served, possibly with spoons. The meat will be in the centre of the dish under vegetables. It is eaten last, often being divided and distributed by the host. Don't eat too much because what often appears to be the main course is actually the first of two or three! Be ready for some strong encouragement to continue eating even after you're full – your host wants to make sure you feel welcome. The phrase *llah yzh"äl lbaraka*, 'may God bring (you) a blessing', is a polite way of saying you've had enough.

Meals

We would like to ...	... بغينا
bgheena ...	
have breakfast	نفطرو
nfetro	
have lunch	نتغداو
nteghddaw	
have dinner	نتعشاو
nt"shaw	

At the Restaurant

We would like a table for
four please.
بغينا واحد الطابلة ديال ربعة عفاك
*bgheena waHed ttaabla
dyal rbe"a "afak*

Please bring me ...
عفاك جيب لي...
*"afak **zh**eeblee ...*
   the menu
المينو
     lmeenoo
   a glass of water
واحد الكاس ديال الما
     *waHed lkas dyal
lma*
   the bill
الحساب
     lHsab

Do you have ...?
واش عندكم ... ؟
wash "ndkm ...?
Is service included in the bill?
واش السرفيس داخل ف الحساب ؟
*wash serbees daxel
felHsab?*

I cannot eat ...
ما نقدرش ناكول ...
manqdersh nakool ...
   meat
الحام
     lHam
   eggs
البيض
     *lba**i**d*
   sugar
السكر
     ssookkar

This isn't cooked well
  enough.
  *hadee matalybash
  mezyan*

هادى ماطايبش مزيان

At the Market

How much for ...?
  bshHal ...?

ب شحال ... ؟

Give me a kg of ... please.
  *"tainee waHed lkeeloo
  dyal ... "afak*

عطيني واحد الكيلو ديال ...
عفاك

I don't want that one.
  mabgheetsh hadeek

مابغينش هاديك

Please give me that other one.
  *"afak "tainee hadeek
  laxoora*

عفاك عطيني هاديك الاخرة

Meat

beef	بجرى
begree	
chicken	دجاج
dzhazh	
ground beef	كفتة
kefta	
heart	قلب
qelb	
lamb	غنمي
ghenmee	
liver	كبدة
kebda	
meat	لحم
lHem	
pork	حلوف
Heloof	
sausage	سوسيس
sooseees	

Seafood

anchovy	شطون
shton	
cod	لامورى
lamooree	
eel	صمطة
semta	
lobster	لانجوس
laangos	
mussel	مول
mool	

sardine *serdeen*	سردين
sea carp *qrb*	قرب
shrimp *qalmroon*	قيمرون
sole *sol*	صول
squid *calamar*	كالامار
tuna *ton*	طون
whiting *merla*	مرلة

Vegetables

artichoke *qooq*	قوق
cabbage *krom*	كروم
carrot *xeezoo*	خيزّو
cauliflower *sheefloor*	شيفلور
celery *krafes*	كرافس
coriander *qesbor*	قصبور
cucumber *xyar*	خيار
eggplant *denzhal*	دنجال

garlic *tooma*	تومة
green pepper *felfla*	فلفلة
green beans *loobeeya*	لوبية
lettuce *xss*	خص
mushroom *feggee"*	فجيع
olive *zeetoon*	زيتون
onion *besla*	بصلة
parsley *m"ednoos*	معدنوس
peas *zhelbana*	جلبانة
potato *btaataa*	بطاطة
pumpkin/squash *ger"a Hemra*	جرعة حمرة
radish *fzhel*	فجل
red pepper *fefla Hemra*	فلفلة حمرة
tomato *mataisha*	مطيشة
turnip *left*	لفت
vegetables *xôdra*	خضرة

Fruit

apple *teffaH*	تفاح
apricot *meshmash*	مشماش
banana *banan*	بنان
cherries *Hebb lemlook*	حب الملوك
date *tmer*	تمر
fig *kermoos*	كرموس
fruit *fakeeya*	فاكية
grapes *"neb*	عنب
lemon *Hamed*	حامض
orange *leemoon*	ليمون
peach *xoox*	خوخ
pear *boo"weed*	بوعويد
plum *berqoq*	برقوق
pomegranate *remman*	رمان
prickly pear *kermoos lhendeeya*	كرموس الهندية
raisins *zbeeb*	زبيب

strawberries *toot*	توت
watermelon *dellaH*	دلّاح

Dairy Products

butter milk *lben*	لبن
butter *zebda*	زبدة
cheese *fromazh*	فروماج
ice cream *laglas*	لاجلاس
milk *Hleeb*	حليب
yoghurt *danoon*	دانون

Drinks

beer *beera*	بيرة
black tea *atay nnegro*	اتاى نجرو
coke *kooka*	كوكة
cold water *lma berd*	الما بارد
hot water *lma sxoon*	الما سخون

juice *"aasair*	عاصير
milk *Hleeb*	حليب
mint tea *atay benna"na"*	اتاى ب النعناع
soft drink *monaada*	موناضة
wine *shrab*	شراب
coffee ... *qehwa ...*	قهوة...
with milk *belHleeb*	ب الحليب
black *keHla*	كحلة
with a little bit of milk *mherresa*	مهرّسة

Condiments

hot sauce	حرور	
Hroor		
jam	كنفيتور	
konfeetoor		
mustard	موتارد	
mootard		
oil	زيت	
zeet		
olive oil	زيت العود	
zeet l"ood		
pepper	لبزار	
lebzaar		
salt	ملحة	
melHa		
sugar	سكر	
sookkar		

Spices

cinnamon	قرفة	
qerfa		
clove	قرنفل	
qronfel		
cumin	كمون	
kamoon		
ginger	سكن جبير	
*sken **zhbeer***		
hot pepper	فلفلة حرّة	
felfla Harra		
paprika	فلفلة حمرة	
felfla Hamra		

saffron *za"fran*	زعفران
sesame **zhenzhlan**	جنجلان

Other Food

barley *sh"air*	شعير
bread *xoobz*	خبز
chips *btaataa meqleeya*	بطاطة مقلية
biscuits/sweets *Helwat*	حلوات

eggs *baid*	بيض
scrambled *mterrba*	مطرّبة
hard boiled *mslooqa*	مسلوقة
fried *mqleeya*	مقلية

flour *dgeeg*	دجيج
rice *rooz*	روز
salad *shlada*	شلادة
sandwich *kaskroot*	كاسكروت

shish kebab *qetban*	قطبان
soup *soba*	صوبة
wheat *gemH*	جمح

Utensils

cup/glass *kas*	كاس
fork *fershetta*	فرشيطة
knife *moos*	موس
plate *tebsaıl*	طبسيل
spoon *m"elqa*	معلقة

Some Useful Words

boiled *mslooq*	مسلوق
bottle *qer"a*	قرعة
clean *nqee*	نقي
cold *bared*	بارد
delicious *ldeed*	لديد
dirty *mwessex*	موسخ

empty   خاوي
  xawee

fresh   طري
  tral

fried   مقلي
  meqlee

full   عامر
  "amer

hot (spicey)   حرّ
  Harr

hot   سخون
  sxoon

rare   ماطايبش بزّاف
  matalybsh bezzef

raw   خضر
  xder

ripe   طايب
  tayeb

roasted   مشوى
  meshwee

rotten   خامج
  *xame**zh***

sour/unseasoned   مسوّس
  mssoos

stale   قديم
  qdeem

sweet   حلو
  Hlew

warm   دافي
  dafee

well done   طايب مزيان
  ***talyeb* mezyan**

Shopping

When shopping in Morocco you will find that almost every price is open for negotiation. Knowing a bit of Arabic will not only give you a chance to have some fun but may also allow you to get a better price.

When shopping in the open-air markets, the souks, you will be confronted by 'guides', who hang around the entrances and are incredibly tenacious. Taking a 'guide' is probably a good idea for your first and second visits as it's an opportunity to familiarise yourself with the layout of the souk. Agree on a price for the 'guide's' services before you set off. You should also make it clear to the 'guide' before you set off that you may not be buying anything.

Where is ...?	فـين ... ؟
feen ...?	
a small food and dry goods shop	كاين شي حانوت
kayn shee Hanoot	
a tobacco shop	كاينة شي صاكة
kayna shee ssakka	
a bookshop	كاينة شي مكتبة
kayna shee mektaba	
a hardware shop	كاين شي دروجرى
kayn shee droogree	
the open air market	كاين السوق
kayn ssooq	

the fruit and vegetable market *kayn lmarshay*	كاين العارشي

the fish market
  kayn lmarshay
  dyal lHoot
	كاين العارشي ديال الحوت

Do you have ...? *wash "ndkom ...?*	واش عندكم... ؟

English newspapers
    zhzhara'eed
    bnegleezeeya
	الجرائد ب النجليزية

film *lfeelm*	الفيلم
a sheet of paper *waHed lwerqa*	واحد الورقة
stamps *ttnaber*	التنابر

Where can I buy ...? *feen ghadee neshree ...?*	فين غادى نشرى... ؟
soap **ss**aabon	الصابون
maps *lxareetat*	الخرائط
pens *ssteeloowat*	الستيلوات
pencils *lqlooma*	القلوما

Bargaining

Traditionally sellers start off at around double the price they are prepared to accept and buyers start off at less than half that amount. Sellers these days, however, frequently start at triple their acceptable price, so you need to start off at around a quarter that price. The price will quickly drop, although in some places, especially Marrakesh, bargaining is hard and often a charade, giving you the illusion you are getting a bargain. Prices there are generally what local people would regard as ridiculous and you'll have trouble lowering them.

If you wish to maximise your bargaining powers, avoid buying anything while you are with a 'guide', as they often receive up to 40% of the price you pay and so are naturally keen for you to buy a lot.

How much?	ب شحال ؟
bshHal?	
It is too much for me.	بزٵف علي
bezzaf "leeya	
That is very expensive.	غالي بزٵف
ghalee bezzaf	
Give me a reasonable price please.	دير معي واحد التمن مناسب عفاك
deer m"aya waHed ttaman me"qol "afak	
What is the last price?	اخر التمن شحال ؟
axeer taman shHal?	
That is my last price.	اخر التمن ديالي هو هادا
axeer ttaman dyalee hoowa hada	

Is there one cheaper than this? واش كاين واحد رخيص على هادا ؟
wash kayn wahed rxais
"la hada?

Souvenirs & Handicrafts

bag/purse	ساك
sak	
blanket	بطانية
bttaaneeya	
brass	نحاس اصفر
nHas ṣfer	
carpet	زربية
zerbeeya	
copper	نحاس احمر
nHas Hmer	
cup	كاس
kas	
embroidery	طرز
terz	
leather	جلد
zheld	
mirror	مراية
mraya	
pitcher	غراف
ghrraf	
plate	طبسيل
tebsel	
pottery	فخار
fexxar	
tray	صينية
ṣaineeya	
vase/pot	محبق
mHebbeq	

Jewellery

bracelet *debleezh*	دبليج
earrings *twangat*	طوانج
gold *dheb*	دهب
necklace *sensla*	سنسلة
ring *xatem*	خاتم
silver *neqra*	نقرة

Clothing

hat *terboosh*	طربوش
jacket *kebbot*	كبوط
pants *serwal*	سروال
shirt *qameezha*	قاميجة
shoes *sebbat*	صباط
socks *tqasher*	تقاشر
sports shoes *sberdeela*	سبرديلة
sweater *treekoo*	تريكو

Toiletries

soap **sabon**	صابون
razor **zezwar**	نزوار
shampoo **shampwan**	شمبوان
toothpaste **m"zhoon dyal snan**	معجون ديال السنان
toothbrush **sheeta dyal snan**	شيطة ديال السنان
after-shave/perfume **reeHa**	ريحة

Stationery/Bookshop

book **ktab**	كتاب
bookshop **mektaba**	مكتبة
envelope **zhwa**	جوى
magazine **mazhella**	مجلة
newspaper **zhareeda**	جريدة
pen **steeloo**	ستيلو
pencil **qalam**	قلم
sheet of paper **werqa**	ورقة

stamp *tanber*	تانبر
writing pad *blok not*	بلوك نط

Colours

white *by**ed***	بيض
black *kHel*	كحل
blue *zreq*	زرق
brown *qehwee*	قهوى
dark *meghlooq*	مغلوق
green *xder*	خضر
grey *rmadee*	رمادى
light *meftooH*	مفتوح
red *Hmer*	حمر
yellow ***s**fer*	صفر

Weights & Measures

gram *gram*	جرام
kilogram *keeloo*	كيلو

metre *meetroo*	ميترو
centimetre **s**aanteem	سنتيم
litre *leetro*	ليترو
half a litre ne**ss** 'eetro	نص ايترو
a little bit *shee shweeya*	شي شوية

Size & Comparison

big *kbeer*	كبير
bigger than this *kber men hada*	كبر من هادا
too big for me *kbeer "leeya*	كبير علي
small **s**gheer	صغير
smaller than this **s**gher men hada	صغر من هادا
too small for me **s**gheer "leeya	صغير علي
tight *mzeyyer*	مزير
long **t**weel	طويل
too much *bezzaf*	بزّاف

Health

Anyone unfortunate enough to become ill will have no trouble finding the medicine they need at any chemist in a major city. Those requiring a doctor nave the choice of nationally funded health services or private doctors and clinics. You will find the French language valuable when dealing with the Moroccan medical system. Since all doctors are educated in French and prescriptions and instructions for taking medicine are written in it as well, an English-French dictionary or phrasebook will prove useful in an emergency.

In an Emergency

Where is ...?　فين ... ؟
feen ...?
    the hospital　كاين الصبطار
      kayn ssbeetaar
    the chemist　كاين الفرماسيان
      kayn lfaarmasyan
    a doctor　كاين شي طبيب
      kayn shee tbeeb
    a dentist　كاين شي طبيب ديال السنان
      kayn shee tbeeb
      dyal ssnan

Call ...　عيط على ...
  "eyyet "la...
    a doctor　طبيب
      tbeeb

an ambulance *labeelans*	لابيلانس

Take me to the doctor! *wesselnee l ttbeeb!*	وصلني ل الطبيب!

Complaints

I have a headache. *kayderrnee rasee*	كيضرّني راسي
I have a cold. *ana mrewweH*	انا مروّح
I have a fever. *feeya sxana*	فيّ سخانة
I have diarrhoea. *kershee zhareeya*	كرشي جارية

My ... hurts. *katderrnee ...*	كتضرّني ...
hand *yeddee*	يدّى
leg/foot *rezhlee*	رجلي
back *dehree*	ضهرى

Is it broken? *wash mherresa?*	واش مهرّسة؟
Is it sprained? *wash mfdoo"?*	واش مفدوع ؟

Allergies

I am allergic to ... عندى واحد الحساسية مع ...
  "ándee waHed lH-
  saseeya m"a ...

   penicillin البنسلين
    lbeenseleen

   this
    hada (m) هادا
    hadee (f) هادى

Parts of the Body

arm درع
  dre"
back ضهر
  dher
blood دم
  demm
bone عضم
  "dem
chest صدر
  sder
ear ودن
  wden
eye عين
  "een
face وجه
  wzheh
finger/toe صبع
  sbe"
hair شعر
  sh"er

hand	يدّ
yedd	
head	راس
raas	
heart	قلب
qelb	
leg/foot	رجل
rzhel	
liver	كبدة
kebda	
lung	رية
reyya	
mouth	فوم
foomm	
shoulder	كتف
ktef	
skin	جلد
zheld	
teeth	سنان
snan	
throat	حلق
Hleq	
tongue	لسان
lsan	

Medication

Do you have medicine for ...?	واش عندك الدوا ديال... ؟
wash "ndek dwa	
dyal...?	
a headache	الراس
rras	
sore throat	الحلاقم
lHlaqem	

diarrhoea *sshal*	السهال
a stomachache *lm"da*	المعدة
a cold *rrewwaH*	الرواح
a cough *lkeHba*	الكحة

Do I need a prescription? *wash xessnee shee werqa dyal ttbeeb?*	واش خصني شي ورقة ديال الطبيب ؟
How many should I take each time? *sHal men waHda ghadee nakool kool merra?*	شحال من واحدة غادي ناكول كول مرة ؟
How many times per day? *shHal men merra fennhar?*	شحال من مرة ف النهار ؟

Some Useful Words

accident *kseeda*	كسيدة
antibiotics *'enteebeeyooteek*	انتيبيوتيك
aspirin *lasbeereen*	لاسبيرين
baby bottle *rddaa"a*	رضاعة
baby food *makla dyal ddraree ssgaar*	مكلة ديال الدراري الصغار

bandage *fasma*	فاصمة
bite *"eddaa*	عضة
broken *mherres*	مهرّس
burn *Herqa*	حرقة
dangerous *xaataar*	خطار
diabetic *"ândoo ssookkar* (m) *"ândha ssookkar* (f)	عندو السكر عندها السكر
infected *m"effen*	معفن
injection *shooka*	شوكة
laboratory *môxtâbâr*	مختبر
medication *eddawa*	الدوا
nappies *xrooq*	خروق
nurse *fermleeya*	فرملية
pain *Hreeq / wzhe"*	حريق / وجع
poison *semm*	سم
pregnant *Hamla*	حاملة
rash *Hboob*	حبوب

sick   مريض
   mreed
swell (v)   نفخ
   nfex
test (lab)   تحليل
   tHleel
vitamin   فيتامين
   veetameen

Times and Dates

Time

Telling the time in Morocco is fairly straightforward and 'am' and 'pm' are replaced by whole words rather than abbreviations. For example, '8 am' is literallly '8 in the morning', *ttmenya fessbaH;* '2 pm' is '2 in the afternoon', *zhzhoozh fel"sheeya;* '8 pm' is '8 at night', *ttmenya felleel.*

Hours

It is ...   ... هادى

  hadee ...

  1   الوحدة

    lewHda

  2   الجوج

    zhzhoozh

  3   التلاتة

    ttlata

  4   الربعة

    rreb"a

5	الخمسة
lxamsa	
6	الستة
ssetta	
7	السبعة
sseb"a	
8	التمنية
ttmenya	
9	التسعود
tts"ood	
10	العشرة
l"shra	
11	الحضاش
lHdash	
12	الطناش
ttnash	

Minutes

Minutes, as in English, are spoken after the hour. The literal translation will provide a feel for how the system works.

It is ...	هادى ...
hadee ...	
1.05	الوحدة وقسم
lewHda ooqsem	
'one and one five minute period'	
1.10	الوحدة وقسماين
lewHda ooqesmayn	
'one and two five minute periods'	

1.15
lewHda oorbâ"
'one and ¼'

1.20
lewHda ootooloot
'one and ⅓'

1.25
lewHda ooxamsa
oo"shreen
'one and 25'

1.30
lewHeda ooness
'one and ½'

الوحدة وربع

الوحدة وثلت

الوحدة وخمسة وعشرين

الوحدة ونص

1.35 **zhzhoozh** qell xamsa oo"shreen 'two less 25'	الجوج قل خمسة وعشرين
1.40 **zhzhoozh** qell tooloot 'two less ⅓'	الجوج قل تلت
1.45 **zhzhoozh** llaroob 'two less ¼'	الجوج الا روب
1.50 **zhzhoozh** qell qesmayn 'two less two five minute periods'	الجوج قل قسماين
1.55 **zhzhoozh** qell qsem 'two less one five minute period'	الجوج قل قسم

Some Useful Phrases

What time is it? shHal fessa"a?	شحال ف الساعة ؟
It's three exactly. hadee ttlata neeshan	هادى التلاتة نيشان
It's about four. hadee rreb"a teqreeben	هادى الربعة تقريبان
hour sa"a	ساعة
two hours sa"atayn	ساعتين

more than two hours *swaye"*	سوايع
an hour from now *men daba waHed ssa"a*	من دابا واحد الساعة
minute *dqeeqa*	دقيقة
minutes *dqayeq*	دقايق
second *taneeya*	ثانية
seconds *taneeyat*	ثانيات
five minutes *qsem*	قسم
ten minutes *qesmayn*	قسمين
now *daba*	دابا
on time *felweqt*	ف الوقت
late *m"ettel*	معطل
early *bekree*	بكرى
around **zh**wayeh	جوايه
past *lmaada**l***	الماضي
present *lHaade**r***	الحاضر
future *lmoosteqbal*	المستقبل

Days of the Week

Sunday
  nhar lHedd
نهار الحدّ

Monday
  nhar letneen
نهار التنين

Tuesday
  nhar ttlat
نهار التلات

Wednesday
  nhar larb"
نهار الاربع

Thursday
  nhar lexmees
نهار الخميس

Friday
  *nhar **zhzh**em"a*
نهار الجمعة

Saturday
  nhar ssebt
نهار السبت

Some Useful Words & Phrases

today
  lyoom
اليوم

What day is it today?
  shnoo lyoom?
شنو اليوم ؟

yesterday
  lbareH
البارح

day before yesterday
  wellbareH
ولّ البارح

yesterday morning
  *lbareH **fess**baH*
البارح ف الصباح

tomorrow
  ghedda
غدّ

tomorrow afternoon
  ghedda fel"sheeya
غدّ ف العشية

a week from today
  bHal lyoom
بحال اليوم

day
  nhar

نهار

two days
  yoomayn

يومين

three days
  telteeyam

تلتيام

day after tomorrow
  b"d ghedda

بعد غدٲ

this week
  had l'oosboo"/sseemana

هاد الاسبوع / السيمائة

two weeks
  zhoozhdel'asabee"/desse
  emanat

جوج د الاسابيع / السيمانات

next week
  l'oosboo" llee **zh**ay

الاسبوع لي جاى

last week
  l'oosboo" llee fat

الاسبوع لي فات

Months

Morocco operates on two calendar systems: the standard Western, or Gregorian, and the Muslim calendar. In general all business and government affairs are conducted by the Western calendar and this is the one that you will need to know. The months are listed here.

The Muslim calendar, used in Morocco mainly for religious holidays, consists of a 354 day year divided into 12 lunar months. A day is added to the last month 11 times in every 30 years, so that in a century the Muslim calendar differs from the Gregorian calendar by just over two years. The first day of the first year corresponds to 15 July 622 AD, the year in which Mohammed and his followers migrated from Mecca to Medina.

The only month of the Muslim calendar that you will need to

be aware of is Ramadan, the traditional month of fasting. From sunrise to sunset each day Muslims refrain from eating, drinking, smoking and other worldly pleasures unless they are ill, pregnant, nursing, travelling, below the age of puberty or otherwise unable. Obviously this causes major disruptions in the pattern of daily life. Businesses usually open mid-morning and close about 4 pm. During the day activity slows down considerably only to increase in the evening as the cafes and streets often remain full until after midnight. While Ramadan can present problems for travellers, in many ways it is an exciting time to be in the country. The religious significance combined with the festive atmosphere in the evenings and many special foods make it a favourite time of year for many Moroccans.

One word of advice during Ramadan, be sensitive to those who are fasting during the day. When possible try not to eat, drink or smoke in public and women should make an effort to dress conservatively.

January *zhanveeyeh*	جانفيي
February *fevreeyeh*	ففري
March *mars*	مارس
April *abreel*	ابريل
May *mayyoo*	مايو
June *yoonyoo*	يونيو
July *yoolyooz*	يوليوز

August *ghoosht*	غوشت
September *sebtamber*	سبتمبر
October *'ooktoober*	اكتوبر
November *noovamber*	نفمبر
December *deesamber*	ديسمبر

Seasons

winter *shtwa*	شتوة
spring *rbee"*	ربيع
summer *saif*	صيف
autumn (fall) *xreef*	خريف

Some Useful Words & Phrases

a month *shher*	شهر
two months *shehrayn*	شهرين
three months *telt shhoor*	تلت شهر
this month *had shshhar*	هاد الشهر
last month *shshhar llee fat*	الشهر لي فات

next month *shshhar llee zhayee*	الشهر لي جاى
a year *"am*	عام
two years *"amayn*	عامين
three years *telt sneen*	تلت سنين
this year *had l"am*	هاد العام
next year *l"am llee zhay*	العام لي جاى
last year *l"am llee fat*	العام لي فات

Numbers

Due to its colonisation by France, Morocco uses the standard Western numerical symbols rather than those normally associated with Arab countries.

Cardinal Numbers

1		واحد
	waHed	
2		جوج
	zhoozh	
3		ثلاثة
	tlata	
4		ربعة
	reb"a	
5		خمسة
	xamsa	
6		ستة
	setta	
7		سبعة
	seb"a	
8		تمنية
	tmenya	
9		تسعود
	tes"ood	
10		عشرة
	"shra	
11		حضاش
	H**d**aash	

115

12 *tnaash*	طناش
13 *teltaash*	تلطاش
14 *rbe"taash*	ربعطاش
15 *xamstaash*	خمسطاش
16 *settaash*	سطاش
17 *sbe"taash*	سبعطاش
18 *tmentaash*	تمنطاش
19 *tse"taash*	تسعطاش
20 *"shreen*	عشرين
21 *waHed oo"shreen*	واحد وعشرين

22		تنين وعشرين
tnayn oo"shreen		
23		تلاتة وعشرين
tlata oo"shren		
30		تلاتين
tlateen		
40		ربعين
reb"een		
50		خمسين
xamseen		
60		ستين
setteen		
70		سبعين
seb"een		
80		تمنين
tmaneen		
90		تسعين
tes"een		
100		مية
mya		
200		ميتين
myatayn		
300		تلت مية
teltmya		
400		ربع مية
rbe"mya		
500		خمس مية
xemsmya		
600		ست مية
settemya		
700		سبع مية
sbe"mya		

800	تمن مية
temnemya	
900	تسع مية
tse"mya	
1000	الف
alf	
2000	الفين
alfayn	
3000	تلت الاف
telt alaf	
10,000	عشرة الاف
"shra alaf	
100,000	مية الف
meyat alf	
one million	مليون
melyoon	
two million	جوج د الملاين
zhoozh *delmlayn*	
one billion	مليار
melyar	

Multiples

To form multiples simply string the appropriate numbers together, separating them with *oo*.

225	ميتين و خمسة و عشرين
myatayn ooxamsa	
oo"shreen	
1989	الف و خمس مية و تسعود و تمنين
alf ootse"meyya	
oots"ood ootmaneen	

Ordinal Numbers

first *loowwel*	لْوّل
second *tanee*	ثاني
third *talet*	ثالت
fourth *rabe"*	رابع
fifth *xames*	خامس
sixth *sades*	سادس
seventh *sabe"*	سابع
eighth *tamen*	ثامن
ninth *tase"*	تاسع
tenth *"asher*	عاشر

the first bus *lkar lloowwel*	الكار اللّوّل
the third street *zzenqa ttalta*	الزنقة الثالتة

Some Useful Words

count (v) *Hseb*	حسب
equal *bHal bHal*	بحال بحال

½   نص
  *ne**ss***

¼   ربع
  rooboo"

per cent   ف المية
  felmya

Vocabulary

A

accident	كسيدة
kseeda	
address	عنوان
"nwen	
advice	نصيحة
naasalHa	
aeroplane	طيارة
talyaara	
after	من بعد
men b"d	
afternoon	عشية
"sheeya	
after-shave/perfume	ريحة
reeHa	
again	عاود تاني
"awed tanee	
age	عمر
"mer	
agriculture	فلاحة
feelaHa	
air-conditioning	كليمتيزسيون
kleemateezaseeyon	
air mail	ب الطيارة
bettalyaara	
all	كول شي
koolshee	

alone, by myself *boowHdee*	بوحدي
also *kadaleek*	كذالك
always *deema*	ديما
America *amreeka*	امريكا
and *oo-*	و
angry *ghe**d**ban*	غضبان
animal *Hayawan*	حيوان
another one *waHed axoor*	واحد اخر
apple *teffaH*	تفاح
approximately *tqreeban*	تقريبا
around ***zh**wayeh*	جوايه
arrival *w**s**ol*	وصول
art *fenn*	فنّ
artist *fennan*	فنان
ashtray *tfaya*	تفايه
ask (v) *sewwel*	سوّل

asleep *na"es*	ناعس
Australia *astraaleeya*	استراليا
awake *fayeq*	فايق

B

back **dh**er	ضهر
bag/purse *sak*	ساك
baggage *baga**zh***	بكاج
banana *banan*	بنان
bandage *fa**s**ma*	فاصمة
bank *baanka*	بانكة
barber *Hellaq*	حلاق
basket *sella*	سلة
bathroom *beet lma*	بيت الما
bathtub *Hemmam*	حمام
battery *batree*	باترى
beach *lapla**zh***	لبلاج

beans, green	لوبية
loobeeya	
beautiful	زوين
zween	
because	على قبال
"la qeebal	
bed	ناموسية
namooseeya	
bedroom	بيت النعاس
beet nn"as	
bee	نحلة
neHla	
beef	بجرى
begree	
beer	بيرة
beera	
before	قبل ما
qbel ma	
behind	مور
mor	
better	احسن
Hessen	
between	ما بين
ma been	
bicycle	بشكليطة
beshkleetaa	
big	كبير
kbeer	
bird	طير
tair	
biscuits/sweets	حلوات
Helwat	

blanket *b*ttaaneeya	بطانية
bleed (v) *seyyel ddemm*	سيل دم
blood *demm*	دم
boat *flooka*	فلوكة
boil (v) *sleq*	سلق
boiled *mslooq*	مسلوق
bone "*dem*	عضم
book *ktab*	كتاب
bookshop *mektaba*	مكتبة
border *Hdada*	حدادة
bored *meqnot*	مقنوط
both *bzhoozh*	بجوج
bottle *qer"a*	قرعة
boulevard *sharee"*	شارع
bowl *zlafa*	زلافة
box *sendoq*	صندوق

box (cardboard) *kartoona*	كرطونة
boy *weld*	ولد
bracelet *debleezh*	دبليج
brass *nHas sfer*	نحاس اصفر
bread *xoobz*	خبز
breakable *eeqder eetherres*	يقدر يتهرس
breakfast *ftor*	فطور
bridge *qentra*	قنطرة
bring (v) *zheeb*	جيب
broken *mherres*	مهرّس
broom *shettaaba*	شطابة
brother *ax*	اخ
brown *qehwee*	قهوى
brush *sheeta*	شيتة
building *bnee*	بني
burn *Herqa*	حرقة

bus *kar*	كار
but *walakeen*	ولكين
butter *zebda*	زبدة
butterilk *lben*	لبن
buy (v) *shree*	شرى

C

cabbage *krom*	كروم
calm *hanee*	هاني
camel **zh**mel	جمل
Canada *kanada*	كندا
candle *shma"a*	شمعة
car **t**omobeel	طوموبيل
careful! *redd balek!*	ردّ بالك!
carpet *zerbeeya*	زربية
cat *meshsh*	مش
centimetre **s**aanteem	سنتيم

chair *koorsee*	كورسي
change **s**e*rf*	صرف
cheap *rxai***s**	رخيص
cheese *froma***zh**	فروماج
chemist *lfaarmasyan*	الفرمسيان
chicken *d***zh**a**zh**	دجاج
children *wlad*	ولاد
chocolate *shooklaa**t***	شوكلاط
cigarettes *garroowat*	جارّوات
cinema *seeneema*	سينيمة
clean *nqee*	نقي
clear, understood *saafee*	صافي
coffee *qehwa*	قهوة
coke *kooka*	كوكة
cold *bared*	بارد
cold (sickness) *mrewweH*	مروّح

cold water *lma bared*	الما بارد
colour *loon*	لون
come! *azheel*	اجي!
comfortable *mreyyeH*	مريح
commerce *teezhara*	تجارة
complaint *shekwa*	شكوة
congratulations *mbrook*	مبروك
cook (v) *teyyeb*	طيب
copper *nHas Hmer*	نحاس احمر
corner *qent*	قنت
cough *keHa*	كحة
count (v) *Hseb*	حسب
country *blad*	بلاد
country market *sooq*	سوق
countryside *badeeya*	بادية
cow *begra*	بجرة

crossroad *kerwazma*	كروازمة
crowded *zHam*	زحام
cup/glass *kas*	كاس
curtain *xameeya*	خامية
customs official *deewaanee*	ديواني

D

damp *fazeg*	فازك
dangerous *xaataar*	خطار
dark **d**lem	ضلم
dark (colour) *meghlooq*	مغلوق
date *tareex*	تاريخ
day *nhar*	نهار
delicious *ldeed*	لديد
desert **s**eHra	صحرا
diarrhoea *kersh zhareeya*	كرش جارية
different *mextalef*	مختلف

difficult *s"aib*	صعيب
dinner *"sha*	عشا
dirt *traab*	تراب
dirty *mwessex*	موسخ
do (v) *dar*	دار
doctor *tbeeb*	طبيب
dog *kelb*	كلب
donkey *Hmar*	حمار
door *bab*	باب
dress (n) *keswa*	كسوة
dress (v) *lbes*	لبس
drop (v) *teyyeH*	طيح
drink (v) *shreb*	شرب
drunk (adj) *sekran*	سكران
dry (adj) *nashef*	ناشف
dry (v) *nshef*	نشف

dull	حافي
Hafee	
dust	غبرة
ghôbra	
duty	واجب
wazheb	

E

each (one)	كل واحد
kool waHed	
ear	ودن
wden	
early	بكرى
bekree	
earrings	توانج
twaneg	
east	شرق
sherq	
easy	سهل
sahel	
Eat!	كول!
kool!	
economic	اقتصادى
qteesaadee	
educated	قارى
qaree	
education	تعليم
te"leem	
eggs	بيض
baid	

electricity **do**	ضو
embassy seefaara	سيفارة
embroidery **terz**	طرز
empty xawee	خاوى
engineer moohendees	مهندس
England anglateera	انجلترا
enough kafee	كافي
entrance dexla	دخلة
envelope **zh**wa	جوى
equal bHal bHal	بحال بحال
essential **d**aroree	ضرورى
Europe ooroba	اوروبا
even so wexxa dak shee	وخة داك شي
evening "sheeya	عشية
everything kool shee	كل شي
exact **s**HeeH	صحيح

example *meetal*	ميتال
excuse (n) *"der*	عدر
excuse me/I am sorry *smeH leeya*	سمح لي
expensive *ghalee*	غالي
experience *tezhreeba*	تجريبة
extra *zayed*	زايد
eye *"eyn*	عين

F

fabric *toob*	توب
face *wzheh*	وجه
factory *mämel*	معمل
faint (v) *sxef*	سخف
fair *mnaseb*	مناسب
fake *mzwwer*	مزوّر
fan *reyyaHa*	رياحة
far *b"aïd*	بعيد

farm	فيرمة
feerma	
fast (adj)	دغية
dgheeya	
fast (v)	صام
saam	
father	والد
waleed	
faucet (tap)	روبيني
roobeenee	
fear	خوف
xoof	
few	قليل
qleel	
film	فيلم
feelm	
find (v)	لجا
lga	
finger/toe	صبع
sbe"	
finish!	كمل!
kemmell	
fish	حوت
Hoot	
flour	دجيج
dgeeg	
flower	نوارة
noowwara	
flight	طيارة
talyara	
fly (insect)	دبانة
debbana	

follow *tbe"*	تبع
food *makla*	مكلة
foot **rzhel**	رجل
foreigner *'azhnabee*	اجنبي
forest *ghaba*	غابة
fork *fershetta*	فرشيطة
fountain *xôssa*	خصة
fourth *rooboo"*	روبوع
fresh **traɪ**	طرى
fried *meqlee*	مقلي
friend **saaHeb**	صاحب
front *qeddam*	قدام
fruit *fakeeya*	فاكية
full *"amer*	عامر
fun *nashaat*	نشاط
future *moosteqbal*	مستقبل

G

game	لعبة
le"ba	
garden	جاردة
zharda	
garlic	تومة
tooma	
germ	ميكروب
meekroob	
German	الماني
almanee	
Germany	المانية
almaneeya	
gift	هدية
hdeeya	
girl	بنت
bent	
give!	عطي !
"ta!	
glass	جاج
zhazh	
glass (drinking)	كاس
kas	
glasses (eye)	نضاضر
*n**d**aader*	
glue	لصاق
lsaaq	
go away	سير ف حالك
seer fHalek	
goat	معزة
me"za	
gold	دهب
dheb	

good *mezyan*	مزيان
goodbye *bessalama*	ب السلامة
government *Hookooma*	حكومة
gram *gram*	جرام
grape *"neb*	عنب
grass *rbee"*	ربيع
green *xder*	خضر
guardian *"ssas*	عساس
guest **d**a*lf*	ضيف
guide (n) *geed*	جيد
gum *mska*	مسكة

H

habit *"ada*	عادة
hair *sh"r*	شعر
half *ne**ss***	نص
hammer *mterqa*	مطرقة

hand	يد
yedd	
handmade	ب اليد
belyedd	
happy	فرحان
ferHan	
harbour	مرصة
mersa	
hat	طربوش
terboosh	
head	راس
raas	
health	صحة
seHHa	
hear (v)	سمع
smô	
heart	قلب
qelb	
heat	صهد
sehd	
heavy	تقيل
tqeel	
help	مساعدة
moosa"ada	
help me!	عاوني !
"awennee!	
here	هنا
hna	
hire/rent (v)	كرا
kra	
historical ruins	اثار
'atar	

holiday *"tla*	عطلة
honest *m"qool*	معقول
horse *"wd*	عود
hospital **s**beetaar	صبطار
hot *sxoon*	سخون
hot (spicey) *Harr*	حرّ
hot water *lma sxoon*	الما سخون
hotel *ootall*	اوطيل
hour *sa"a*	ساعة
how? *keefash?*	كيفاش ؟
hungry **zh**ee"an	جيعان
Hurry up! *serbee!*	سربي!
husband *ra**zh**l*	راجل

I

ice *tel**zh***	طج
ice cream *laglas*	لجلاس

idea
  feekra فكرة

identification
  te"reef تعريف

immediately
  feessa" في الساع

information
  me"loomat معلومات

injection
  shooka شوكة

inside
  daxel داخل

inspector
  moofetteesh مفتش

insurance
  laasoraans لاصورانص

interesting
  mooheem مهم

island
  zhazeera جزيرة

J

jacket
  kebbot كبوط

jail
  Hebs حبس

jam
  konfeetoor كنفيتور

jewellery
  beezhoo بيجو

job/work
  xedma خدمة

joke (v) ضحك
dHek

journalist صحافي
saaHaafee

juice عصير
"a**s**alr

K

key ساروت
saroot

kilogram كيلو
keeloo

kiss (n) بوسة
boosa

kitchen كوزينة
koozeena

knife موس
moos

knock (v) دقّ
deqq

know (v) عرف
"**r**ef

L

lake ضاية
daya

lamb غنمي
ghenmee

language لغة
loogha

last, final اخير
axeer

late *m"ettel*	معطل
law *qanoon*	قانون
lawyer *mooHamee*	محامي
learn (v) *t"ellem*	تعلم
leather **zheld**	جلد
left *leeser*	ليسر
leg/foot *rzhel*	رجل
lemon *Hame**d***	حامض
length **tol**	طول
less *qell*	قلّ
letter *bra*	برة
lay down *tekka*	تكة
life *hayat*	حياة
lift (elevator) *sensoor*	سنسور
light **do**	ضو
light (colour) *meftooH*	مفتوح

light bulb *bola*	بولة
like (v) *bgha*	بغا
like (similar) *bHal*	بحال
Listen! *sm"!*	سمع!
little bit *shee shweeya*	شي شوية
lock *qfel*	قفل
long *tweel*	طويل
Look! *shoof!*	شوف!
loose *metlooq*	متلوق
lost *talf*	تلف
loud *mzhehhed*	مجهد
love *Hebb*	حب
luck *zher*	زهر
luggage *Hwayezh*	حوايج
lunch *ghda*	غدا

M

magazine *mazhella*	مجلة
mailman *faktor*	فاكتور
make (v) *saweb*	صاوب
male *dker*	دكر
man *razel*	رجل
many *bezzaf*	بزۡاف
map *xareeta*	خاريتة
market *sooq*	سوق
marriage *zhwazh*	جواج
married *mzhewwezh*	مجوج
matches *wqaid*	وقيد
meaning *m"na*	معنى
meat *lHem*	لحم
message *meesaazh*	ميساج
metre *meetroo*	ميترو
milk *Hleeb*	حليب

mint tea *atay benna"na"*	اتاى ب النعناع
mirror *mraya*	مراية
mistake *ghalta*	غالطة
money *floos*	فلوس
monkey *qerd*	قرد
month *shher*	شهر
moon *gmra*	جمرة
more *kter*	كتر
mosque **zh**ame"	جامع
mother *waleeda*	والدة
motorcycle/moped *motor*	موطور
mountain **zh**bel	جبل
mouth *foomm*	فوم
mud *ghees*	غيس
mule *bghel*	بغل
museum *metHef*	متحف

music
   mooseeqa

mutton
   ghenmee

موسيقة

غنمي

N

name
   smeeya

nationality
   zhenseeya*

near
   qreeb

necessary
   lazem

necklace
   sensla

needle
   eebra

neighbour
   zhar*

never
   "emmer ma

new
   zhdeed*

news
   xbar

newspaper
   zhareeda*

next
   zhay*

night
   leela

سمية

جنسية

قريب

لازم

سنسلة

ابرة

جار

عمر ما

جديد

خبار

جريدة

جاى

ليلة

no	لا
la	
nobody	حتى واحد
hetta waHed	
noise	صداع
sda"	
north	شمال
shamal	
nose	نيف
neef	
nosey	فضولي
*f**d**olee*	
not	ماشى
mashee	
not yet	ما زال
mazal	
nothing	والو
waloo	
now	دابا
daba	
number	رقم
raqem	
nurse	فرملية
fermleeya	

O

ocean	بحار
bHar	
of	ديال
dyal	
office	مكتب
mektab	

oil *zeet*	زيت
OK *waxxa*	وخة
old *qdeem*	قديم
olive *zeetoon*	زيتون
olive oil *zeet l"ood*	زيت العود
on *"la*	على
on time *felweqt*	ف الوقت
once *merra waHeda*	مرّة واحدة
only *gheer*	غير
open (adj) *meHlool*	محلول
open (v) *Hell*	حلّ
operation (medical) *"amaleeya*	عملية
orange *leemoon*	ليمون
order *taalaab*	طالب
ordinary *"adee*	عادي
original *'eslee*	اصلي

other | اخر
axoor

outside | برّة
berra

over | فوق من
fooq men

P

package | باكية
bakeeya

pain | حريق
Hreeq

paint | صباغة
sbagha

palace | قصر
qser

pants | سروال
serwal

paper | ورقة
werqa

paper (wrapping) | كاغيت
kagheet

park (v) | وقف
wqef

past | ماضي
maadai

pay (v) | خلص
xelles

pen | ستيلو
steeloo

penalty | خطية
xtaiya

pencil *qalam*	قلم
people *nas*	ناس
pepper *lebzaar*	لبزار
percent *felmya*	ف المية
petrol *leesans*	ليصانص
pharmacy *farmasyan*	فرمسيان
picture *tesweera*	تصويرة
piece **terf**	طرف
pig *Helloof*	حلوف
pillow *mxedda*	مخدّة
pitcher *ghrraf*	غرّاف
place *blaasa*	بلاصة
plant *nabat*	نبات
plate **tebsail**	طبسيل
please *"afak*	عفاك
pocket **zheeb**	جيب

poison *semm*	سم
policeman *booleesee*	بوليسي
poor *meskeen*	مسكين
possible *yemken*	يمكن
post office *bosta*	بوسطة
pot *tenzhra*	طنجرة
potato *btaataa*	بطاطا
pottery *fexxar*	فخار
pregnant *Hamla*	حاملة
prescription *werqa dyal ttbeeb*	ورقة ديال الطبيب
president *ra'ees*	رئيس
pretty *zween*	زوين
problem *mooshkeel*	مشكل
pronunciation *nôtq*	نطق
pull (v) *zhbed*	جبد
push (v) *dfô*	دفع

Q

quality
  zhooda
جودة

quantity
  "adad
عدد

question
  soo'al
سؤال

quickly
  dgheeya
دغية

quiet
  mhedden
مهدن

R

radio
  raadyoo
راديو

rain
  shta
شتا

rash
  Hboob
حبوب

raw
  x**der**
خضر

razor
  zezwar
زنوار

read (v)
  qra
قرا

ready
  moo**zh**ood
موجود

receipt
  faktoora
فاكتورة

red
  Hmer
حمر

refrigerator *tella**zh**a*	تلاجة
region *naHeeya*	ناحية
rent (v) *kra*	كرا
repair (v) ***s**laH*	صلح
repeat (v) *awed*	عاود
return (v) ***rzh**â"*	رجع
rice *rooz*	روز
rich *ghanee*	غاني
right (direction) *leemen*	ليمن
right (of people, etc) *Heqq*	حقّ
ring *xatem*	خاتم
ripe ***t**ayeb*	طايب
river *wad*	واد
road ***t**raiq*	طريق
roasted *meshwee*	مشوى
rock *He**zh**ra*	حجرة

roof **st**aaH	صطاح
room beet	بيت
rope qennba	قنبة
rotten xame**zh**	خامج
round m**d**wwer	مضوّر
rubbish zbel	زبل
run (v) **zh**ra	جرا

S

salad shlada	شلادة
salt melHa	ملحة
same bHal bHal	بحال بحال
sand remla	رملة
sandal sandala	سندلة
sandwich kaskroot	كاسكروت
sausage soosees	سوسيس
scared xayf	خايف

scenery *mender*	منضر
school *medraasa*	مدرسة
screw *vees*	فيس
screwdriver *ternoovees*	تورنوفيس
sea *bHer*	بحر
seat *kôrsee*	كرسي
second (unit of time) *taneeya*	ثانية
sell (v) *ba"*	باع
send (v) *saifet*	صيفط
sentence *zhoomla*	جملة
service *serbees*	سربيس
sew (v) *xeyyet*	خيط
shade *dell*	ضلّ
shampoo *shampwan*	شامبوان
shave (v) *Hessen*	حسن
sheet *eezar*	ازار

ship *baboor*	بابور
shirt *qameezha*	قاميجة
shoe lace *seer*	سير
shoes *sebbat*	صباط
shop *Hanoot*	حانوت
shop for groceries (v) *tqedda*	تقضنا
short *qsair*	قصير
shower *doosh*	دوش
shut *msdood*	مسدود
sick *mreed*	مريض
signature *tôwqee"*	توقيع
silver *neqra*	نقرة
sit down! *gles!*	جلس!
skin *zheld*	جلد
sleep *n"sa*	نعسة
slow down! *beshweeya "leek!*	ب شوية عليك !

small	صغير
sgheer	
smell (v)	شمّ
shemm	
smoke a cigarette (v)	كما
kma	
snake	حنش
Hensh	
snow	تلج
telzh	
soap	صابون
saaboon	
socks	تقاشر
tqasher	
soft	رطب
rteb	
soft drink	موناضة
monaada	
some	شي
shee	
something	شي حاجة
shee Hzha	
sometimes	بعض المرات
bâdlmerrat	
son	ولد
weld	
song	غنية
ghôneeya	
sour/unseasoned	مسوس
mssoos	
south	جنوب
zhanoob	

speak (v) *tkellem*	تكلم
spend the night (v) *bat*	بات
spoon *m"elqa*	معلقة
stairs *droozh*	دروج
stale *qdeem*	قديم
stamp *tanber*	تانبر
star *nezhma*	نجمة
stay (v) *gles*	جلس
stomach *kersh*	كرش
stop! *Hbes*	حبس!
stop light **do** *lHmer*	ضو الحمر
stop sign *stop*	سطوب
straight *neeshan*	نيشان
strange *fsheeshkel*	ف شي شكل
street *zenqa*	زنقة
string *xeyyet*	خيط

student *taaleeb*	طالب
sugar *sookkar*	سكر
suitcase *baleeza*	باليزة
sun *shemsh*	شمش
sweater *treekoo*	تريكو
sweet *Hlew*	حلو
swim (v) *"oom*	عوم

T

table *taabla*	طابلة
tablet (medicine) *faneed*	فانيد
tailor *xeyyat*	خياط
tape *skaatsh*	سكاتش
taste (v) *daq*	داق
tax *daaraiba*	ضريبة
taxi *taaksee*	طاكسي
tea *atay*	اتاى

teacher *'oostad*	استاد
teeth *snan*	سنان
telegram *teeleegram*	تيليجرام
telephone *telefon*	تيليفون
television *telfaza*	تلفزة
thankyou *shôkran*	شكرا
theatre *mesreH*	مسرح
thick *ghlaid*	غليض
thin *rqaiq*	رقيق
thing *Hazha*	حاجة
thirst *"tesh*	عطش
thirsty *"âtshan*	عطشان
thread *xeyt*	خيط
throat *Helq*	حلق
ticket *werqa*	ورقة
tight *mzeyyer*	مزير

tired *"eyyan*	عيان
today *lyoom*	اليوم
toilet *beet lma*	بيت الما
tomorrow *ghedda*	غد٣
tongue *lsan*	لسان
toothbrush *sheeta d ssnan*	شيطة د السنان
top *fooq*	فوق
torch *beel*	بيل
touch (v) *qaas*	قاص
tourist *sa'eeH*	سائح
towel *fota*	فوطة
town *mdeena*	مدينة
trade (v) *tbadel*	تبدل
train *masheena*	ماشينة
translation *terzhama*	ترجامة
travel (v) *saafer*	صافر

tree	شجرة
shezhra	
truck	كاميو
kameeyoo	
true	حقيقي
Haqeeqee	
turn!	ضور!
dorl	
turn (n)	نوبة
nooba	

U

umbrella	مضل
mdell	
under	تحت من
teHt men	
understand (v)	فهم
fhem	
understood	مفهوم
mefhoom	
university	جامعة
zhamee"a	
untie (v)	حلّ
Hell	
upset/mad	مقلق
mqelleq	
use (v)	ستعمل
ste"mel	

V

valley	واد
wad	

vase
meHbeq محبق

vegetables
xdra خضرة

very
bezzaf بزّاف

view
mender منضر

village
dwaar ضوار

vitamin
veetameen فيتامين

vomit (v)
tqeyya تقيا

W

wait
tsenna تسنا

waiter
garson جارسون

wake up (v)
faq فاق

wall
Heyt حيط

want (v)
bgha بغا

warm
sxoon سخون

wash
ghsel غسل

wash (clothes)
sebben صبن

watch (n) *magana*	مكنة
Watch out! *"ndak!*	عندك!
water *lma*	الما
waterfall *kaskad*	كسكاد
watermelon *dellaH*	دلّاح
wave (ocean) *moozha*	موجة
way *traiq*	طريق
wear (v) *lbes*	لبس
weather *Hal*	حال
week *'oosboo"*	اسبوع
weigh (v) *wzen*	وزن
weight *wzen*	وزن
west *gherb*	غرب
What? *shnoo?*	اشنو؟
wheel *rwaida*	رويضة
When? *eemta?*	امتى؟

Where?	فـين ؟
feen?	
Which?	اش من ؟
ashmen?	
Who?	شـكون ؟
shkoon?	
whole	كامل
kamel	
Why?	علاش؟
"lash?	
wife	مرة
mra	
wind	ريح
reeH	
window	شرجم
sherzhem	
wine	شراب
shrab	
with	مع
m"a	
woman	مرة
mra	
woods/forest	غابة
ghaba	
wool	صوف
so*f*	
word	كلمة
kelma	
work	أخدمة
xedma	
world	عالم
"alam	

write (v)
  kteb
كتب

X

x-ray
  raadyo
راديو

Y

year
  "am
عام

yellow
  sfer
صفر

yes
  eeyeh
ايه

yesterday
  lbareH
البارح

yoghurt
  danoon
دانون

young
  sgheer
صغير

Z

zero
  sfer
صفر

zipper
  sensla
سنسلة

zoo
  Hadeeqa delHayawan
حديقة د الحيوان

Emergencies

Help!
   "teqnee!

عتقني !

Emergency!
   'erzhens / mestâ"zhel!

ارجانس/ مستعجل !

There's been an accident!
   ooq"ât kseeda!

وقعت كسيدة !

Call a doctor!
   "ayyet "la shee tbeeb!

عيط على شي طبيب!

Call an ambulance!
   "ayyet "la ssayyara del'as"af!

عيط على السيارة د الاسعاف !

Go away!
   seer fHalek!

سير ف حالك!

I'll call the police!
   gaadee n"eyyat "la lboolees!

غادى نعيط على البوليس!

Thief!
   sheffar!

شفار !

Fire!
   l"âfeeya!

العافية!

Help me please!
   "awennee "afak!

عاوني عفاك!

Where is the police station?
   feen kayna lkomesareeya?

فين كاينة الكومسارية ؟

Where is the toilet?
   feen kayn ttwaalet?

فين كاينة التواليت ؟

Someone robbed me!
  serreq leeya shee
  waHed!
	سرق لي شي واحد!

Call the police! *"ayyet "la lboolees!*	عيط على البوليس!
My ... was stolen. *tesreq leeya ... dyalee*	سرق لي ...ديالي

I've lost my ...
  twedder leeya (s)
  twedderoo leeya (pl)
	توضر لي ...
	توضرو لي ...

bags *lHwayezh*	الحوايج
money *lfloos*	الفلوس
travellers' cheques *sheekat seyaHeeya*	شيكات سياحية
passport *lpaspoor*	الباسبور

I am ill.
  ana mraid (m)
  ana mraida (f)
	انا مريض
	انا مريضة

I am lost. *telfat "leeya traiq*	تلفت علي الطريق

Could I use the telephone?
  waxxa stâ"melt
  teeleefon?
	واخا ستعملت التلفون ؟

I wish to contact my
  embassy/consulate.
  **bgeet nttasel
  bessefara/belqonsoleyya
  dyalee**

بغيت نتصل ب السفارة/
القنصلية ديالي

I speak (English)
  **kantkellem
  (negleezeyya)**

كنتكلم (نجليزية)

I have medical insurance.
  **"ândee lasoorans dyal
  ssHHa**

عندى لاسورانس ديال الصحة

I understand.
  fhemt

فهمت

I don't understand.
  mafhemtsh

ما فهمتش

I'm sorry. I apologise.
  smeH leeya

سمح لي

Contact (next of kin)
  **ttasel b (shee
  waHed men l"aa'eela)**

اتصل ب
(شي واحد من العائلة)

Where can you find out
HOW to get a Laotian visa in Bangkok?

***WHERE** to go birdwatching in PNG?*

***WHAT** to expect from the police if you're robbed in Peru?*

***WHEN** you can go to see cow races in Australia?*

In the Lonely Planet Newsletter!

Every issue includes:

X *a letter from Lonely Planet founders Tony and Maureen Wheeler*

X *a letter from an author 'on the road'*

X *the most entertaining or informative reader's letter we've received*

X *the latest news on new and forthcoming releases from Lonely Planet*

X *and all the latest travel news from all over the world*

To receive the FREE quarterly Lonely Planet Newsletter, write to:
Lonely Planet Publications, PO Box 617, Hawthorn 3122, Australia
Lonely Planet Publications, Embarcadero West, 112 Linden St, Oakland, CA 94607, USA

Morocco, Algeria & Tunisia
a travel survival kit

Morocco, Algeria and Tunisia are linked historically and culturally, but each offers the traveller something unique. Discover the splendour of Islamic architecture in the imperial cities of Morocco; visit Tunisia's world-famous Roman ruins; or take a trip across the Algerian Sahara – one of the greatest adventures on earth.

This practical guide takes you from bustling souks to peaceful oases, and will help travellers reap the rewards of getting off the beaten track.

Lonely Planet travel guides are available round the world.
For a copy of our current booklist or a list of our distributors write to:
Lonely Planet, PO Box 617, Hawthorn, Vic. 3122, Australia
Lonely Planet, Embarcadero West, 112 Linden St, Oakland, CA 94607, USA

Travel Survival Kits

Alaska
Argentina
Australia
Baja California
Bali & Lombok
Bangladesh
Bolivia
Brazil
Burma
Canada
Central Africa
Chile & Easter Island
China
Colombia
East Africa
Ecuador & the Galapagos Islands
Egypt & the Sudan
Fiji
Hawaii
Hong Kong, Macau & Canton
Iceland, Greenland & the Faroe Islands
India
Indonesia
Islands of Australia's Great Barrier Reef
Israel
Japan
Jordan & Syria
Karakoram Highway
Kashmir, Ladakh & Zanskar
Kenya
Korea
Madagascar & Comoros
Malaysia, Singapore & Brunei
Maldives & Is. of the East Indian Ocean
Mauritius, Réunion & Seychelles
Mexico
Micronesia
Morocco, Algeria & Tunisia
Nepal
New Caledonia
New Zealand
Pakistan
Peru
Philippines
Rarotonga & the Cook Islands
Samoa
Solomon Islands

Sri Lanka
Tahiti & French Polynesia
Taiwan
Thailand
Tibet
Tonga
Turkey
West Africa
Yemen

Shoestring Guides

Africa on a shoestring
Eastern Europe on a shoestring
North-East Asia on a shoestring
South America on a shoestring
South-East Asia on a shoestring
West Asia on a shoestring

Trekking & Walking Guides

Bushwalking in Australia
Tramping in New Zealand
Trekking in the Indian Himalaya
Trekking in the Nepal Himalaya
Trekking in Turkey
Trekking in Spain

Phrasebooks

Brazilian
Burmese
Chinese
Egyptian Arabic
Hindi/Urdu
Indonesia
Japanese
Korean
Moroccan Arabic
Nepal
Papua New Guinea
Pilipino
Quechua
Sri Lanka
Swahili
Thai
Tibet
Turkish

And Also

Travel with Children

Lonely Planet travel guides are available around the world.
For a copy of our current booklist or a list of our distributors write to:
Lonely Planet, PO Box 617, Hawthorn, Victoria 3122, Australia
Lonely Planet, Embarcadero West, 112 Linden St, Oakland, CA 94607, USA